SOFTWARE PROJECT HEALTH
AN EPIC RETOLD

Paramu Kurumathur

PM Power Consulting

INDIA • SINGAPORE • MALAYSIA

Notion Press

Old No. 38, New No. 6
McNichols Road, Chetpet
Chennai - 600 031

First Published by Notion Press 2018
Copyright © Paramu Kurumathur 2018
All Rights Reserved.

ISBN 978-1-64324-770-0

This book has been published with all efforts taken to make the material error-free after the consent of the author. However, the author and the publisher do not assume and hereby disclaim any liability to any party for any loss, damage, or disruption caused by errors or omissions, whether such errors or omissions result from negligence, accident, or any other cause.

No part of this book may be used, reproduced in any manner whatsoever without written permission from the author, except in the case of brief quotations embodied in critical articles and reviews.

Disclaimer

The story, all names, characters and incidents portrayed in this production are fictitious. No similarity with actual persons (living or deceased), fictional characters, names, places, buildings, events, locales, incidents, businesses and products is intended or should be inferred.

Reviews

Overall, Software Project Health: An Epic Re-told, certainly fulfills its promise. The core sections on engineering and execution excellence are particularly outstanding and reflect the collective experience of PM Power practitioners for which there is no substitute. Software Project Health: An Epic Re-told is a book well worth reading…

– **Ashok Soota, Executive Chairman, Happiest Minds Technologies**

This book is a valuable contribution to the software project management literature. Through the definition of a new project health framework, it addresses the need to fill the gap left by using metrics alone to manage a project and not having a mechanism for continuous monitoring of projects. The "style" of the book "An epic retold" is a refreshing and absorbing.

– **Prof. S. Sadagopan, Director, IIIT, Bangalore**

The author has intelligently used the characters of the Mahabharata to lucidly narrate the concepts of Software Project Health. The multi-dimensionality of any large software project has been explained in simple terms of Vital Signs, appealing to any practitioner. Integrating Customer Connect and Engaged Management is novel not usually touched upon by existing project management literature.

– **Krishna Prasad, Director and Country Manager, AS & UX Segment, Aptiv India**

Software Project Health – An Epic retold" has great insights from a real practitioner's on-the-ground experiences. A required surveillance tool in the armory of all Project Managers in the era of digital disruption. With its unique approach of assessing project health and forecasting outcomes, the book enables stakeholders to gain new insights into executing projects. A must read!

— **L. Ravichandran, President and Chief Operating Officer, TechMahindra**

The book Software Project Health: An Epic re-told makes for very interesting reading. Complex concepts and recipes for lasting success in project management are made very easy by this excellent compilation from PM Power practitioners. Presented superbly like a story in a conversational style, the book is very different from conventional project management books. The vital signs for assessing project health illustrated in the book are very holistic and comprehensive. The key aspects have been discussed thoroughly in each of the sections, and summarization of action points at the end of each section is done extremely well. The book is a must read for every project and program management professional.

— **Ramakrishnan Sudarshanam, Divisional VP – IT, United Breweries Ltd.**

Contents

Foreword ix

Preface xiii

Acknowledgements xxi

Cast of Characters xxiii

Chapter 1	Introduction	1
Chapter 2	Customer Connect	38
Chapter 3	Goal Focused Team	86
Chapter 4	Engineering Excellence	101
Chapter 5	Execution Excellence	134
Chapter 6	Engaged Management	186
Chapter 7	Continuous Improvement	215
Chapter 8	Programs	224
Chapter 9	Conclusions	231
Chapter 10	Epilogue	239

Are You Ready to Implement the Framework?		*249*
Appendix A	*Making of the Book and the Tool*	*251*
Appendix B	*The Project Health Framework*	*254*
Appendix C	*About PM Power Consulting*	*272*
About the Author		*273*

Foreword

All of us who have been involved in project management must, at some stage, have received a nasty surprise. A project, which has been green till yesterday, suddenly turns red. Maybe it was red all along, but we didn't perceive the same. Another variant of the shock is when a project is seemingly all green, but a customer calls to convey he wants to review the relationship.

Software Project Health: An Epic Re-told is a timely book that seeks to put an end to such shocks by introducing a predictive approach, which assures customers of only positive and repeatable outcomes.

The essence of *Software Project Health: An Epic Re-told* is to focus on 6 vital signs and in each of these look beyond quantitative metrics alone and gather qualitative inputs from all the stakeholders. The 6 vital signs conceived by the experienced author are:

- Customer Connect
- Goal-Focused Team
- Engineering Excellence
- Execution Excellence
- Engaged Management and
- Continuous Improvement

The vital signs are comprehensive enough to build a holistic view of project health and an objective way to let the customer know what is happening and get customer inputs. At the end of each section, the key learnings or action points are succinctly tabulated.

Software Project Health: An Epic Re-told is presented with a backdrop of the Mahabharata where the city of Hastinapura decides to implement a security system that would ensure complete protection from their enemies.

This leads to an easy conversational style, which makes the book different from the usual "what and how to do" books. The conversations between the Pandavas and between Krishna and Arjuna also bring in the "why" dimension to changes needed to ensure project excellence.

However, for the impatient reader like myself, occasionally, I found myself going straight to the learnings and no doubt missed the context of many points. But, the patient reader will definitely be more rewarded.

Project execution has been a perennial problem in the software world. The traditional challenges have been exacerbated in the present digital age; for example, the need for unearthing unstated customer needs, quick adoption of new technologies and, as a consequence, multi-skilling of teams. There is also the need for continuous value-add to the customer who rightly expects value-add beyond just project deliverables and meeting SLAs. I am happy to note that the author has taken note of these newer challenges and provided insights on these throughout the book.

PM Power Consulting deserves appreciation for sponsoring the book and having its team members actively contribute and support the author in writing this book.

I gather from the PM Power team that they have further developed the concepts in the book to a formal mechanism for assessing project health and forecasting outcomes, including an automated 360-degree self-assessment by project stakeholders. This tool will no doubt be of significant value – one that would help many software delivery organizations in improved project delivery and predictable performance in future projects.

Overall, *Software Project Health: An Epic Re-told* certainly fulfills its promise. The core sections of engineering and Execution Excellence are particularly outstanding and reflect the collective experience of PM Power practitioners for which there is no substitute. *Software Project Health: An Epic Re-told* is a book well worth reading, and its learnings are to be captured in the minds of all involved with successful project delivery.

– Ashok Soota
Bangalore
Executive Chairman, Happiest Minds Technologies
22/03/2018
https://www.happiestminds.com/about-us/leadership-teams/ashok-soota/

Preface

We were having our regular Thursday meeting. This meeting provided the platform for each partner or consultant of my organization (PM Power Consulting Pvt. Ltd. aka PM Power) to update the others on their status and plans. Three of our partners had been busy over the past couple of months working on a framework to assess project health. This framework was the brainchild of Anantha Natarajan, who had always been wanting to come up with a way to assess the true health of a software project.

Ananth was not satisfied that the regular status updates of the project managers, using quantitative metrics, actually gave the true status of a project. How do you account for the intuition that, as a reviewer, you get as you sit through a 'green' project review, that something is wrong? Why is the customer making dissatisfied noises when the project manager has consistently supplied them (and you) with 'green' status reports?

This was what set Ananth to rope in two of my colleagues S. Srinivasan and S. Sivakumar into a cabal (with a combined experience of around a 100 years) to create a project health assessment framework. This cabal, almost coming to blows among themselves, worked for over a month to get the framework ready. This framework was tested on many critical and large-sized projects in the captive software development center of a leading US automotive software company. The test was a success, and it was decided to take the framework and recommended improvements to other organizations to assess the true health of their projects.

At that Thursday meeting that I was talking about, Anantha presented the framework, the story of its creation, the result of the test with the automotive software company and future plans.

This was what the framework was about: The key to the health of a project is the implementation of good practices. A 'healthily' developed product is one that has good practices implemented during all stages of its development. A product that is developed through a project that is healthy at all stages always assures positive outcomes. The recipient of the product is also assured that the provider (the developer of the product) can repeat this success in future product development. The framework is worked by grouping these practices into 'vital signs' and using them for assessing the health of a project.

Quantitative metrics alone would not be able to accurately predict the health of a project. Qualitative inputs from all the stakeholders are also needed. Different stakeholders, such as the customer, the team, the project manager and delivery management may have different perspectives about the status of the project at any time. In fact, different stakeholders may have different perspectives on the same quantitative measurement! Quantitative metrics should, therefore, be viewed jointly with stakeholder perspectives from their respective vantage points.

Sensing the true status or health of a project, at any point in time, will help project managers get an early warning of troubles ahead, apply timely actions where needed and steer the project on a path of Continuous Improvement.

The writer in me was fascinated by Anantha's presentation on the above concepts. Here was something that we could, and should, write a book about. The book could talk about starting from practices and their manifestations, grouping them into vital signs and how the vital signs could be used to assess the health of a project. This is how I started on this project – writing a book about the project health framework.

The immediate question that came to my mind was how to make the book interesting and not read like a documentary or a boring textbook. Write it like writing a novel! What kind of setting? Why not the setting of the old Indian epic, the Mahabharata? It was settled.

The city of Hastinapura decides to implement a security system that would ensure complete protection from their enemies. They shortlist two companies, the Pandavas and the Kauravas and give them both the requirements of the product suite to be developed. Whoever delivers the better defense system at the end of the stipulated period of two years, or earlier, would get rewarded.

'Better system' means not just the quality of the delivered product suite. It also means the ability to demonstrate, during the development process, an ongoing assurance of achieving the desired outcomes at the end of the program. The customer, if at any time during the development feels that the program is not progressing properly, has the option of terminating the agreement.

The Pandavas are sure that a product that is developed in an environment that follows rigorous practices and is confident of the final outcomes at every stage will prove to be the better one. It will be more robust. There will be less defects and problems. And, this would also ensure that the defense department will look at the Pandavas as an organization with which they could have an ongoing relationship.

The Kauravas, on the other hand, decide to stick with their usual status reporting and forecasting mechanisms even though their spies tell them what is cooking in the Pandava camp. They would "somehow" manage customer expectations and audits!

Arjuna, a new hire, is the Pandavas' program manager for a program code-named Kurukshetra. Krishna, an external consultant, is hired to coach Arjuna through the program implementation.

Arjuna is diffident and is consumed by self-doubt. Is he equal to this great task of delivering the Kurukshetra Program? His main worry is that he will not be able to ascertain the true status of the constituent projects of his program. Without this, how will he deliver a quality program and products on time? His concern is how he will be able to judge the health of his constituent projects on a continual basis. He feels he will fail in this.

Krishna comes to Arjuna's rescue and mentions the broad outline of PM Power's health framework and how Arjuna can allay his doubts through expanding and applying the framework in the context of projects in the Kurukshetra Program.

It is thus that Arjuna, with Krishna by his side, launches on a journey of discovery talking to project managers, team members, account managers, his boss (Yudhishthira) and the customer (Air Marshal Bharata) to evolve the framework from the PM Power-supplied foundations of six vital signs (Customer Connect, Goal-Focused Team, Engineering Excellence, Execution Excellence, Engaged Management and Continuous Improvement) into a comprehensive set of underlying components and manifestations.

So, you may ask, "How is this framework different from others such as CMMi and ISO?" Here is how:

- The health framework is not certification-oriented or an assessment of capability or maturity for delivering future projects or marketing the organization; it is about here and now and how to deliver better on current projects
- It is comprehensive, including all aspects: Customers, project team, engineering, project management and delivery management
- The approach to assessing health is 360-degree, covering all key stakeholders

In addition to developing the framework, the book also talks of a formal mechanism to periodically capture the above 360-degree stakeholder perspectives and forecast the outcomes of a project. These forecasts can serve to help correct a wayward project, at any stage of the project. What poor health of a vital sign indicates is that the practices underlying that vital sign are unsatisfactory.

The framework and the tool's design and inference engine are based on the essence of many years of PM Power experience in guiding projects and delivery organizations. The framework and tool have been validated in many organizations using many projects. They are being refined as more data points come in.

I realized that writing a business book like a novel was no easy task. How do I make specialized and may-be-dry topics interesting to a large audience? For this, I created various scenarios and used one scenario each for a vital sign/component/manifestation. I have tried to convey some real-world kind of experience through these scenarios. Hopefully, this will appeal to readers.

I spent a total of around eight months elapsed time to complete this book. At the same time, I was also writing my first novel – a murder mystery, set in Vedic times! Switching from one context to another was quite a difficult task.

The primary source of this book is the framework created by Anantha and others. I have followed this faithfully. I also consulted many books and articles on project management, Agile, program management, etc. Details of these references are given at the end of the book.

As I told you before, I followed the framework faithfully, or I was made to follow this faithfully. My friend and colleague, Sivakumar (fondly known as Big Shiv), who acted as the Product Owner of this book writing effort, held a whip over me to ensure that I did not wander off. If this book is a success, it is primarily due to him. He meticulously reviewed every version of the book and made valuable suggestions. Many a time, he suggested scenarios. And many a time, he rewrote things I had written.

Others who contributed to the book include Ananth, Gopal, JV, Sivaguru, Srinivasan and others in PM Power consulting.

Finally, many thanks to my parent organization, PM Power, who has sponsored this book and continues to support it.

I hope readers enjoy reading this book as much as I enjoyed writing it.

Paramu Kurumathur,
Bangalore
Author and Writer,
21/02/2018
Partner and Principal Consultant, PM Power Consulting

Acknowledgements

The Author, on behalf of PM Power Consulting expresses his gratitude to the following people, who have been kind enough to extend their support and assistance in ideation, illustrations, and publishing.

1. Krishna Prasad, who provided many inputs during the ideation phase and is a strong supporter and endorser of this effort.
2. Shraddha Kanojia, who provided the wonderful illustrations that brought life to the narration.
3. Dattatri Salagame and S. Sridhara who provided good insights in the early stages.
4. All the endorsers of the book for their encouraging words.
5. notionpress staff, who guided us through every step of the publication process and ensured that we brought out the book on time.

Cast of Characters

Character	Role
Abhimanyu	Project Manager of Chakravyuha
Air Marshal Bharata	Program Manager of Kurukshetra in the Hastinapura Defense Department
Amba	Sales Manager for Kurukshetra – Pandava Solutions
Ambalika	Account Manager for Kurukshetra – Pandava Solutions
Anantha	Project Management Expert from PM Power. Author (with others) of a paper on project health
Bhanumati	Project Manager of Parivartanavyuha
Bharatavarsha	A country
Bhima	Quality Assurance Director of Pandava Solutions
Bhishma	Chairman of Kaurava Software
Chakravyuha	A component project of Kurukshetra
Chitrangada	Legal Manager of Kurukshetra Program in Pandava Solutions

Character	Role
Damayanti	Leader of the testing team of Samyojana
Dhrtarashtra	CEO of Kaurava Software
Divodasa	Program Manager in another software company. Friend of Arjuna
Draupadi	Chairperson of Pandava Solutions
Drishtadyumna	Marketing Manager of a large chip manufacturing company. Arjuna's brother-in-law
Duryodhana	Chief Operating Officer of Kaurava Software
Gardabhavyuha	A component project of Kurukshetra
Ghatotkacha	A project manager
Hastinapura	City. Capital of Bharatavarsha. Kurukshetra Program was for its defense
Hidimbi	An engineer in the Indravyuha Project
Indravyuha	A component project of Kurukshetra
Karna	Works Manager of the largest automobile plant in the country
Kaurava Software	Software development organization
Krishna	A coach
Krishna Prasad	CEO of Temple of Apollo Self-Moving Systems
Krpa	Testing Team Leader of Kurmavyuha Project

Krtavarman	Team Leader of the performance engineering group of Kurmavyuha Project
Kurmavyuha	A component project of Kurukshetra
Kurukshetra	Program for the defense of Hastinapura
Madri	Administration Officer of the Kurukshetra Program
Nakula	Project Manager of Kurmavyuha
Pandava Solutions	Software development organization
Parivartanavyuha	A component project of Kurukshetra
Prajapati	Chief Technical Architect of the Kurukshetra Program
Priyamvada	An officer in the Pandava Program Management Office
Revati	Project Admin of Samyojana Project
Saatyakeyi	A project manager
Sahadevi	Project Manager of Samyojana
Samyojana	A component project of Kurukshetra
Sanjaya	Dhrtarashtra's assistant
Shakuni	Program Management Officer of Kaurava Software
Sharmishtha	A Module Leader of Kurmavyuha project
Sudas	Program Manager in another software company. Friend of Arjuna

Character	Role
Tilottama	Lead Test Engineer of Indravyuha Project
Urvashi	Head of Corporate Security – Pandava Solutions
Uttara	A Module Leader in Chakravyuha Project
Vidura	An Officer of Kaurava Solutions
Yayati	Project Manager of Indravyuha Project
Yudhishthira	Vice President of Pandava Solutions in charge of Kurukshetra Program

Chapter 1

Introduction

Dhrtarashtra Asks for the Status of the Kurukshetra Program

"Sanjaya, what are Pandava Solutions doing in Kurukshetra? And what are we doing?" Dhrtarashtra sat in his large office and asked. "Will we be able to do better than them and win?"

Sanjaya said, "Well, it has been a month since the program started, and we were doing a bit better till now. However, I am not very sure that that is going to last. The Pandavas have let go of their program manager who was running the show so far and have managed to assign a super program manager, Arjuna, to take on the program. And, Krishna himself, of Krishna Consulting, has agreed with Yudhishthira that he will coach Arjuna on the job."

Dhrtarashtra was the CEO of Kaurava Software, one of the largest software companies in Hastinapura. He was talking to his assistant, Sanjaya. They were sitting in Dhrtarashtra's slick paneled office. It had a great view of the Yamuna and the fort. The smell of freshly brewing coffee filled the room. They already had a cup of coffee each in their hands.

Dhrtarashtra was surprised. He took a sip. "Krishna himself?"

"Yes, though most of his team will work for us, Krishna himself will work for Pandava Solutions. We have a staff-for-hire contract with them while Pandavas have a consultant contract."

The defense department of Hastinapura, called the "department," wanted a large software product suite developed that would ensure complete security of Hastinapura from her enemies. Codenamed "Kurukshetra" by the department, this program would be one of the largest software development programs ever executed in the whole continent of Bharatavarsha. Given the mission-critical nature of the project, the department used a novel approach for vendor selection. They shortlisted two companies, Pandava Solutions, known as the Pandavas, and Kaurava Software, known as the Kauravas, and gave them both the requirements of the product suite to be developed.

The department had a certain pot of money in their budget. Whoever delivered the better defense system at the end of the stipulated period of two years would get three-quarters of the pot of money, and the other company would get a quarter.

"Better system" meant not just the quality of the delivered product suite. It also meant the ability to demonstrate, during the development process, an ongoing assurance of achieving the desired outcomes at the end of the program. The department, if at any time during the development, felt that the program was not progressing properly, had the option of terminating the agreement, after the payment of the termination fee.

The Kauravas and the Pandavas agreed to this, and the development "war" started in earnest. It would be a prestigious program for both the companies. A big portion of their revenue would come from this program if they won the contest.

Duryodhana, the COO of the Kauravas, had gone to the consultant firm Krishna Consulting to hire some people for the program. So had Yudhishthira, the VP of Delivery of the Pandavas. Duryodhana managed to hire most of the top managers for his program before Yudhishthira could. However, Yudhishthira bagged a great prize. Krishna himself agreed to coach the new program manager of the Pandavas during the program.

Sanjaya said, "Now, one month into the program, both the companies have their full contingent of people and resources ready, and the program is going full steam ahead."

Sanjaya told Dhrtarashtra that he had a spy among the Pandavas. He would report to him what was going on there.

"Who are the main project managers assigned to this large program in Pandava Solutions?"

The phone rang. Sanjaya picked it up, listened for a while and said, "Vidura on line. He needs to talk to you urgently."

Dhrtarashtra took the phone and put it to his ear. He kept saying, "Yes," "Yes," and finally said, "Send along the papers. I will look at it and send you my approval." He put the phone down.

He told Sanjaya to continue.

"Yudhishthira is the Vice President in charge of the program. Arjuna, as program manager, reports to him. As you may know, the Kurukshetra Program consists of a number of projects delivering key constituents of the defense system. The defense system will be built in an incremental fashion integrating these constituents as they become available. The project managers in charge of the largest of these constituent projects who report to Arjuna are: Nakula, Sahadevi, Abhimanyu, Ghatotkacha and Saatyakeyi. There are many other project managers also in charge of development of other constituents."

Dhrtarashtra said, "I know their chairperson, Draupadi, well. We used to work together long ago."

Sanjaya then listed for Dhrtarashtra the managers and the chief engineers of Kaurava.

Dhrtarashtra said, "Okay. Good, you can report to me every week on the progress of the two organizations."

"Yes, sir."

When he was going out of Dhrtarashtra's office, Vidura was hurrying in with some papers in his hand.

Yudhishthira Talks to Arjuna and Gives Him Charge of the Program

Yudhishthira was sitting in his large office. He was a very busy man. His calendar was almost always full. Yudhishthira's office was on one of the upper floors of the large building that housed more than three thousand engineers of Pandava Solutions. In fact, the Pandava Solutions office was across a large thoroughfare from Kaurava Software's office. People in one office could literally see people in the other office.

Arjuna waited outside while Yudhishthira was wrapping up his previous meeting. He had to wait for some time. Yudhishthira's assistant offered him coffee and cookies while he was waiting.

Once his meeting was over, Yudhishthira's assistant indicated to Arjuna that he could go in. After the usual greeting, Yudhishthira offered him coffee. Arjuna declined. He was already full from the cookies!

Yudhishthira did not waste time. "Arjuna, welcome to this prestigious program. I see this as a great opportunity for you in your career. If we do this program well, our division will be the toast of our organization."

Arjuna said, "Thanks. I hope I will be able to live up to your expectations."

Yudhishthira said, "You know that we are in competition with the Kauravas for this program. We are both developing the same product suite in parallel. The defense department will evaluate both at the end and choose the better of the two."

"I know. What is meant by the term 'better system?'"

"Ha, good question. All they have said is that they will choose 'the better system.'"

He continued, "But, they emphasized that the quality of the development practices and quality of the product suite as it developed was as critical as the final deliverable. There will be periodic progress reviews to see which team can provide a greater assurance of a quality outcome. Note one important thing. If at any time during the development the customer feels that the program is not developing properly, they have the option of terminating the agreement."

"Then what criteria can we apply? Of course, we can deliver the product suite to the required quality at the required time. But, what about the practices themselves?"

Yudhishthira said, "I have been thinking about this. Last evening, I had dinner with Krishna Prasad, the CEO of Temple of Apollo Self-Moving Systems. We discussed this at length. The question we asked ourselves was 'Is not the real test whether the product suite delivered meets the required scope and quality on schedule?'"

Yudhishthira continued. "Krishna Prasad then made an interesting observation. He said, 'But, I can assure you that both your product and the Kauravas' product will very likely meet all requirements at the highest quality and will be delivered on time.'"

Arjuna said, "I see what you mean."

Yudhishthira asked, "So, when the quality is equal and when the product has been delivered on time, what other factors will be under consideration?"

Arjuna said, "The health of the development practices."

Yudhishthira said, "Yes, in fact, Krishna Prasad was of the opinion that a product that was developed in an environment that followed rigorous practices and was confident of the final outcomes at every stage will prove to be the better one. It will be more robust. There will be less defects and problems."

Yudhishthira added with emphasis, "If the practices were not rigorous, the resultant product may meet the acceptance criteria but may throw up issues later."

Arjuna said, "And the department is looking at the long term for a preferred partnership."

"Exactly. Even though a winner will need to be declared at the end of the program."

Yudhishthira asked, "What would you think should be some of the practices?"

"Good connection with the customer, for example?"

"Excellent. The defense department will look at us as an organization with which they can have an ongoing relationship. How will they decide that? That is where some of the parameters I talked about come in. As you mentioned, one key element is good connection with the customer and another would be execution practices."

"Okay."

Yudhishthira said, "I have a call with the CEO of a US customer of another project after our meeting. That guy is certainly not happy with the system we delivered. Of course, the system per se is okay, but his gripe is that we did not advise them properly on some of the new technologies that they could have employed. You see the problem? As experts in technology and software development, we should be in a position to advise our customers. This is what we are talking about. You should be able to add value to the customer without their ever asking for it and not just do what they stated they want. Anyway, that project is not your problem. You should concentrate on Kurukshetra. But, we should not end up in the same situation with Hastinapura defense."

He continued, "I am having a meeting with Krishna today. You know Krishna, right? We have hired him to coach you on this program."

"Oh, that would be very helpful. I can do with some coaching on this."

"You know, Arjuna, this is a large program. The management of a large program like this is very challenging. Recognizing that real 'program management' is different from 'management' in general is very important. The competencies required are very different. I know that you have been a project manager and a good all-round manager."

He continued, "As I was saying, being a critical program, taking all stakeholders along is very important. Ensuring good practices in the constituent projects – in planning, risk management and other areas – and also transparency of progress and issues with the customer would increase the connect and cement a basis of trust. To do these, adopting good practices in all areas of program and project governance is important. We hired Krishna to make sure that you get the required guidance to run this large program."

"I am happy about this. I will surely gain from having Krishna as my coach."

Yudhishthira said, "As I mentioned, I am meeting Krishna today. I will discuss with him the concepts we discussed today and ensure that he is fully aware of what needs to be done. This will provide him the background for his coaching."

"Thank you, Yudhishthira. I will ensure that you will not be disappointed."

Yudhishthira said, "I think you should meet Prajapati. He is the chief technical architect of the program. He can give you a rundown of the constituent systems of the defense system."

"Okay. I will do that."

Yudhishthira said, "And, Arjuna, it has been one month since the program started. We brought you in specially because this is going to be a very difficult program to handle, and we felt that the previous program manager, though quite good, was not up to the task of running such a critical program. Though all the projects under the program have started and have been fully resourced, you may want to look at the progress of each of these projects carefully. We felt that we were lagging behind the Kauravas a bit. This is where you come in."

"I will not disappoint you, Yudhishthira."

The Defense System Explained

The next day, Arjuna met up with Prajapati, the chief architect of the Kurukshetra Program. Prajapati explained to Arjuna the key constituents of the system.

He said, "Arjuna, welcome to this program. The defense department has been looking at building such a defense system for a long time now. Only now they have been able to get the necessary funding from the government for this."

Arjuna asked, "Are all the hardware and software components indigenously developed?"

"Well, some of the hardware components are being imported from friendly countries, while some are being developed internally by some of the defense labs. All the software is being developed inside the country. And this is where we come in. Some of the key constituents are as given in this picture. Of course, there are many other components and subsystems. I am just trying to give you an overview. There are also many other systems including housekeeping systems."

Prajapati took out a large sheet of paper that had this diagram.

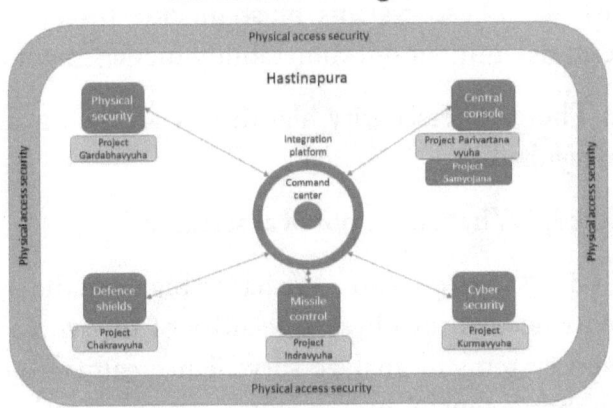

Introduction | 11

Prajapati said, "The defensive shield around Hastinapura is one of the key constituents of the defense system. This includes the radar systems and other detection systems, satellite-based surveillance systems, airborne early warning and control systems, drones, etc."

"The required software for this defense net is being developed in project Chakravyuha."

He continued, "Another key component of the system is the user interface. The user interface of the defense system is quite critical. It should be clear, concise and consistent.

"It should allow for intelligence reading, understanding the current situation, as well as for taking action. You should know what the skies and the terrain around the city looks like. You should be able to launch missiles if needed, etc. Of course, you should not be launching a missile instead of a drone!

"This user-interface is being developed by the project Parivartanavyuha."

Prajapati continued, "Another key component is the security of the system. The system should be shielded completely, and no one should be able to hack into the system. An enemy hacking in could create chaos in the city and country."

Arjuna asked, "These systems must include threat identification, risk assessment, risk mitigation, vulnerability management, etc.?"

"Correct. These cybersecurity algorithms are being developed by project Kurmavyuha."

Arjuna asked, "What about physical security?"

Prajapati said, "Good question. We have a big team that is developing the components needed for physical security of the whole city. Things like recognition systems to analyze surveillance camera outputs, alarm systems and lighting control, access control systems, etc."

"Which project is developing the software for these?"

"Project Gardabhavyuha."

"Okay."

Prajapati said, "The other key constituent is the missile launching and guidance systems. Any incoming enemy missile or aircraft should immediately be intercepted and destroyed."

"The algorithms for this must be very, very complicated."

"They are. Project Indravyuha is handling this development."

Prajapati continued, "And finally, there is the platform for integrating all these key systems. This is being developed under the project called Samyojana."

"Okay. I understand."

Prajapati said, "Well, these are the key systems that are being developed. Of course, as I mentioned earlier, there are many other smaller projects. But, these are the key ones."

"All right. I now have a good, overall idea of the system components and architecture."

Arjuna's Self-doubt

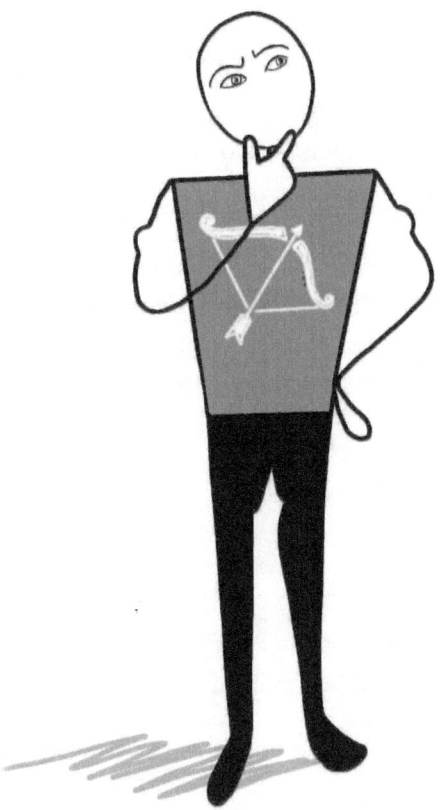

"Am I equal to this great task, Krishna?" asked Arjuna. "Can I deliver Kurukshetra for the Pandavas?"

Arjuna had not worked on such a large program before. But Yudhishthira was confident that Arjuna had the potential to deliver this large program.

When Krishna walked into Arjuna's office that morning, Arjuna seemed a nervous wreck. "Why me?" seemed to be written all over his face. He was drinking a large mug of strong coffee. He seemed to have been suddenly seized by self-doubt.

He said without waiting for Krishna to say anything, "I have only done much smaller programs before. This is the first time I have had such a large program to deliver. If this is not delivered properly, Pandava Solutions will suffer huge losses. Losses mean massive layoffs. Layoffs mean untold misery to employees."

He continued, "And even if we ultimately win the contest, during the progress of the program, I will need to ask my teams to work day and night. I need to learn to become immune to the sufferings of my team members. I have to sacrifice my home life to ensure that this program is delivered properly."

Krishna interjected, "A good program manager should be able to deliver programs without such drastic measures!"

Arjuna was on a roll with his doubts. "I will be the cause of all these problems for so many people. It is better that I resign now and let the organization hire someone better to deliver this program."

Saying thus, he took out a sheet of paper to write out his resignation.

Krishna said, "Whence this thought so unbecoming of you? You have led large programs before. This may be much larger than any program you have so far led, but that does not mean you are unequal to the task."

Arjuna hesitated. He knew there was trouble when Krishna used archaic language!

Krishna continued, "You can and will deliver this program. Pandava Solutions will execute and win Kurukshetra Program. I will guide you and coach you."

Krishna spoke again, "Even if you fail, you will gain great experience. This experience will be valued by this and other companies. You should work without thinking of the result. If you keep worrying about the result – whether you will win or fail – you will not be able to concentrate on the program. Please do not have doubts."

Krishna then asked Arjuna. "What is your main worry? What is the problem that is making you doubt your self-worth?"

Arjuna said, "As the program manager of the program, I should always be on top of the program. I should know what is going on and have the status of the overall program and each constituent project at my fingertips. Is this not right, Krishna?"

"Absolutely! And your worry is not misplaced. Effective assessment of project and program status and taking timely corrective actions can sometimes be quite challenging."

"That is what I am getting at. Well, Krishna, my main worry is that I will not be able to ascertain the true status of the constituent projects of my program. Without this, how will I deliver a quality program and products on time? My concern is: How will I be able to judge the health of my constituent projects on a continual basis? I feel I will fail in this."

He continued, "Based on my previous experience, some of my worry areas are the following."

He listed his potential problems to Krishna.

- The project managers working for me will not be able to recognize symptoms of project problems
- Project managers will try to fix problems by themselves rather than seek expert advice
- Project reviews do not always happen or are not effective
- Project reviews will not be objective
- Process audits will tell only part of the story
- Senior managers will be too busy with general and organizational management activities to provide the required attention to the project
- Customer point of contact – project manager relationship (good or bad) gets in the way in objective satisfaction rating
- Hidden technical and code issues may be waiting to explode
- Teams may become complacent

Krishna said, "Oh, my God! This is a long list of problems that you foresee. Are you not exaggerating the problems? Anyway, most managers go through this self-doubt before they start large projects or programs. What do you think is really missing?"

Arjuna said, "A holistic view of project health, an objective way to let the customer know what is happening and get customer inputs and ongoing and timely guidance to the project managers and other managers."

Krishna said, "You seem to have summarized the issues well. Do not worry. Trust me. I will support you in discovering the solution for these issues."

Krishna spent a lot of time reassuring Arjuna. At the end of this session, Arjuna seemed to have lost some of his diffidence. "I have faith in you, Krishna. I will deliver this program, coached by you."

Krishna said, "Let us meet tomorrow again at the same time. We can look at how to ensure the health of the constituent projects so that you can guide them to reach the highest level of performance possible. I had a long discussion with Yudhishthira yesterday. I am clear as to what he wants."

He continued, "One of the key things that Yudhishthira was talking about was how the Pandavas can deliver a product suite with outcomes expected by the customer. In addition, the product should be the more 'healthily' developed one. This will also give the customer the confidence that your success is repeatable."

Arjuna said, "Yes. Yudhishthira was talking about this."

Krishna said, "Arjuna, can't you see? It is precisely the features that define the health of a project that you are looking for to ensure that a project is doing well! You and Yudhishthira have been thinking along similar lines! What appeared to you as a set of self-doubts appeared to Yudhishthira as a set of parameters to measure our projects with."

Arjuna almost fainted. "Of course! This is a revelation."

"Why don't you think about this? We can discuss this further tomorrow."

Arjuna Meets Draupadi - 360-Degree View of Projects

Draupadi was the chairperson of Pandava Solutions. When she heard that such a large program like Kurukshetra was being handled by her organization, she asked to have a meeting with the program manager, Arjuna. Her office was in another part of town.

Draupadi was one of the old-timers in the software industry. She had started working in software development when punched cards were the medium of input and IBM 370s were the greatest computers. She retired from executive work as the CEO of Pandava Solutions and was now its chairperson. She was also on the board of some of Pandava's sister companies. She was now well over sixty but took an active interest in the strategy and governance of the companies.

Arjuna was a bit diffident about meeting a person at such a high level. He thought that Draupadi would be a bit old-fashioned and thought that he may need to explain some of the current concepts of project and program management.

Arjuna was surprised when he met Draupadi. She was a simple woman with no pretensions. And through the conversation Arjuna was to realize how wrong he was about Draupadi. Far from being an old fogey, she was completely aware of all the modern concepts and techniques.

Arjuna noticed that Draupadi had a small bar in her office. Obviously, she would open it when she had meetings with chairpersons of other organizations and senior officers.

She warmly welcomed Arjuna and asked him to sit down.

After serving him tea, Draupadi asked Arjuna, "Tell me about this Program Kurukshetra. I know that you are new, but…"

Arjuna gave a brief summary of the program and its circumstances, as best as he could.

Draupadi said, "I heard that you have hired Krishna as a coach to help you?"

"Yes, that is correct."

"I know Krishna. I am kind of related to him. He is a good boy."

Arjuna smiled when he heard Krishna being referred to as "boy."

Suddenly Draupadi asked, "Do you have any questions for me?"

Arjuna seized the opportunity. "Madam, one of my key concerns is assessing the health of the constituent projects and bringing in Continuous Improvement. How do I know that things are going well? Can I rely on the usual status reporting systems and what my project managers tell me? Should I install something better given the criticality of the program?"

Draupadi asked, "What do you mean by 'health of the project?'"

Arjuna said, "I mean two things. One, the quality of the delivered product and two, the quality of the development practices itself. I understand that unless both are done well, the project cannot be called a success."

He continued, "It's like when we go to the doctor's for a check-up. So far you have not had a heart attack, but, the way you are living now, eating all those fried things, is showing up in your cholesterol count. This vital sign is not good. You are likely to get a heart attack sometime in the future."

"Yes, you are right. You need to keep your eyes on both these aspects. Otherwise, you may end up delivering an acceptable product, but the customer may not have the confidence that your success is repeatable."

Draupadi said, "One thing that I will advise you to do is to dig into any knowledge base that our Program Management Office has kept. This will give you some idea of why some projects were successful and some were not. I find that many project managers and program managers do not dig into this knowledge base. This may be seen as old-fashioned, but there is a lot to be said about it."

"Thanks, I will look into this and see what I can learn from this."

Draupadi said, "The other thing is this. I understand that these days, customers expect vendors not just to deliver projects as per specifications, but to be innovators and co-creators."

She continued, "This is where your 'connect' with the customer becomes important. Once you establish the right kind of relationship with the customer, this becomes easier to handle. Innovative ideas can easily be moved into the scope and unwanted things moved out. You can then get a win-win situation."

Draupadi then asked, "This is a fixed-price program, of course?"

"Yes, it is. The defense department has a fixed time allotted to the project. Whoever delivers the better product suite at the end of this time period with the must-have constituents and most of the should-have constituents integrated will be the winner and will be given three-quarters of the budgeted pot of money."

"OK. I can understand the peculiar circumstances of this program. However, in most projects, you should be able to convince the customer that Agile + innovation is better than fixed scope and price."

"Yes. Some of the projects within my program are being delivered using the Agile approach. I am less worried about these projects. Agile approaches have some built-in processes and checks to ensure better delivery and outcomes, if the processes are followed correctly. It is the other ones using non-Agile methods that I am more worried about."

Draupadi said, "Arjuna, I don't think that you can take the success of Agile projects for granted, just because they are Agile."

"That's true."

Draupadi said. "You asked the question about the health of the development practices. One key thing I have to say is 'happiest team makes for happiest customer.'"

"How do we ensure 'happiest' team?"

"When I used to be a project manager like you many years ago, during any project review, I used to do a quick flash survey of all the team members. This used to help me get a quick heat-map of the project."

"What is that?"

"For one, I used these surveys to figure out if people were clear on their roles. I also tried to ensure that people could open up and have their problems addressed. Perspectives of individuals are important. Understand them better, and sense what they are telling you and why. Change them for the better."

"Okay."

"It is important to catch any problem upstream, rather than downstream. What you find is that project managers and program managers get more attention from management when they firefight well, not when they ensure that there are no fires. I have fished in these waters, both as the angler and the fish, to know about this!"

Draupadi continued, "One of the best ways to check on the health of an ongoing project is to understand the perspectives of individuals from different vantage points. For example, you may feel that a project is going well – schedules are being met, scope is being realized, quality is okay. And the customer acknowledges this. But still, they are not happy! Similarly, even though the team's performance is good, team members are not happy. So, the real health of a project needs to be measured by understanding the perspectives of different stakeholders on how the project is going. In fact, the best method is a 360-degree view of the project. What do various stakeholders feel? The customer, the team members, the management, the project manager and others."

Arjuna said, "This makes sense. When I talk to Krishna, I can bring this up so that we can tie this whole thing up."

Draupadi continued her advice to Arjuna on team aspects. "One key thing you need to remember with new-age software projects is that sometimes the work-life balance of team members is affected. People work very late over long periods and become unproductive overall. You need to think about this also."

Arjuna said, "Yes, I have been thinking of this and making sure that team members are not put under undue hardship."

Draupadi asked, "Changing the subject, do you have a good sense of the underlying technologies?"

"Not fully. I thought my project managers did. But after talking to them, I think that I need to make an effort to better understand some of the key technologies."

"This is important. If not, you may find it difficult to understand and connect with the teams."

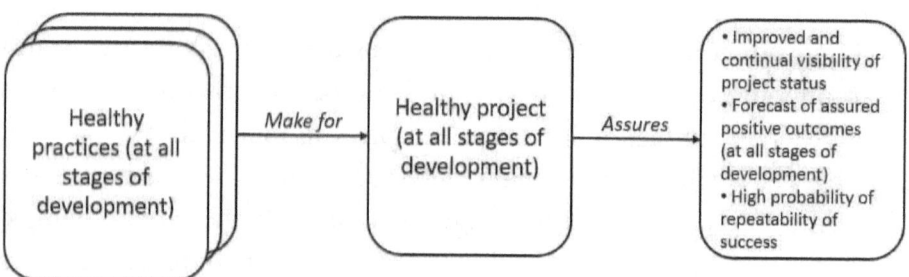

"Yes, I realize that."

Draupadi said, indicating that the meeting was over, "It was great talking to you. I have gained from this meeting. I hope you have too. If at any time during this program you feel you need to talk to me, please feel free to give me a call. I will talk to Yudhishthira and others. You can call me without worrying about protocol."

"Yes, ma'am. Thank you. I enjoyed talking to you, and I learned a lot about managing this program. I will keep you updated on this."

"Okay. Good."

The Six-Fold Approach to Assess Project Health

"With the help of Krishna, I will nail down the factors that make a project healthy, the factors that make a project meet the customers need for inherent quality," thought Arjuna as he walked from his car to his office. He shivered in the cold, but he was excited. He was looking forward to the session with Krishna.

He got himself a coffee and walked to his office saying "hi" to a few colleagues who were already at work.

When he reached his office, Krishna was sitting there waiting for him. He looked at his watch. No, he was not late. Krishna was just early. Arjuna was sure that Krishna was well worth the money they were paying him.

"Hi, Krishna. How are you this morning?"

"Am good. You seem to have become cheerful and confident."

"Yes. My meeting with Draupadi cheered me up. It was a very useful meeting. Now, I cannot wait for our next session of coaching."

Arjuna, who was doing the daily crossword while walking, put down his newspaper and sat down.

Krishna asked, "Well, Arjuna, have you thought about what we discussed last time?"

"Yes, I have."

"What do we need to do?"

Arjuna elaborated.

"The key to the health of a project is the implementation of good practices. A 'healthily' developed product is a product where good practices are implemented at all stages during development. A product that is developed through a project that is healthy at all stages, always assures positive outcomes. The recipient of the product is also assured that the provider (the developer of the product) can repeat this success in future product development.

"Internally sensing the true status of a project, at any point in time, will help project managers apply corrective actions where needed and steer the project on a path of Continuous Improvement.

"This approach will set us apart from our competitor, the Kauravas, and others in the eye of the customer."

Krishna said, "Excellent. You seem to have got the main approach down pat. As far as the first part is concerned, I will coach you and some of the senior project managers. We can request Yudhishthira to hire some more coaches to help the team leaders and the engineers, if needed, later on. We can decide this based on the situation then."

Krishna continued, "Now, let us take the second part. How do we gain this visibility to value-creation and improvement areas you are talking about? Don't regular status updates provide you with this information?"

Arjuna thought and said, "Well all these metrics-based approaches give only quantitative information."

"Is that not what you want?"

"Of course, we need that. But we also need qualitative information. We need to be able get the 'human-experience'-based indicators to accurately read the status of a project's health."

He then updated Krishna on the "vantage points" way of getting a 360-degree evaluation of the project, arising from his conversation with Draupadi.

Krishna said, "Okay. That makes sense. For each project, at any point in its 'existence,' we can do this 360-degree evaluation of the health.

Of course, this method should be supplemented by the metrics-based approaches."

"Certainly."

Krishna said, "But, what are these indicators that measure qualitative aspects of project health? Only yesterday, I was going through a paper written by project management experts Anantha and two of his colleagues of PM Power Consulting of Hastinapura. They have discussed this aspect at length in their paper."

"Oh, good. Somebody has already thought of this. What do they say?"

Krishna thought for a while and said. "The paper is based on the experience of Anantha and his colleagues over their many years of work in various organizations. It seems once Anantha was sitting in a project review, and he realized that the project manager was reporting 'all green,' even while some of the team members were giving indications to the contrary."

Arjuna asked, "Does this happen often?"

Krishna said, "Yes, the most difficult thing is to realize something is going wrong. The paper says that this experience got Anantha thinking. Over the next few months, based on his review of a large number of projects, he formulated an approach to assessing project health. His thinking was that we should be able to list a set of 'manifestations,' which are visible features in which issues can be observed and improvement actions can be applied. We can then group these into a set of components and further group the components into what are called 'vital signs' of a project."

Arjuna was interested. "Vital signs of a project? Much like the vital signs we use to assess the health of a human being?"

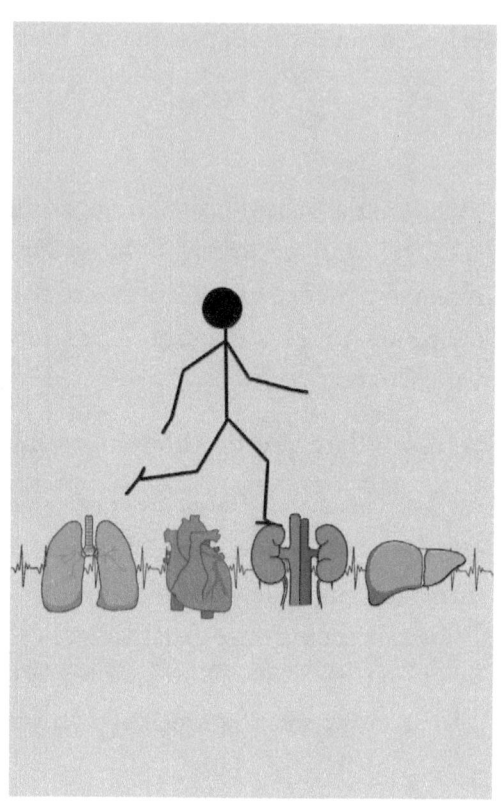

"Yes, exactly."

"Give me an example of this manifestation, component and vital sign."

Krishna referred to the paper, "Well, one manifestation is this: *Regular communication with the customer exists regarding operational status – weekly, monthly, quarterly*. This manifestation and many other similar ones are part of the component *Operational Connect with the Customer*, and this component and other similar components are part of the vital sign *Customer Connect*."

"Ok. This is interesting. So, what Anantha et al are saying is that looking at the set of manifestations comprising Customer Connect will tell you whether that vital sign of the project is healthy. Is that right?"

Krishna said, "Yes, that is right. Other than Customer Connect, the paper lists five more vital signs."

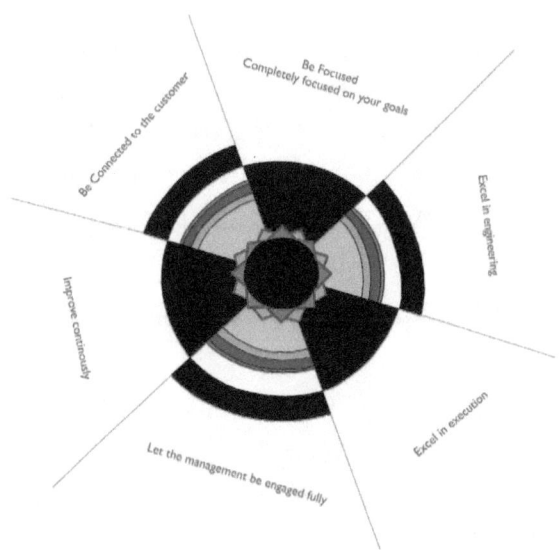

"Oh, okay. This seems to be a good approach. I think I can look at this for our program. Does the paper list all the components and manifestations under these vital signs?"

Vital signs

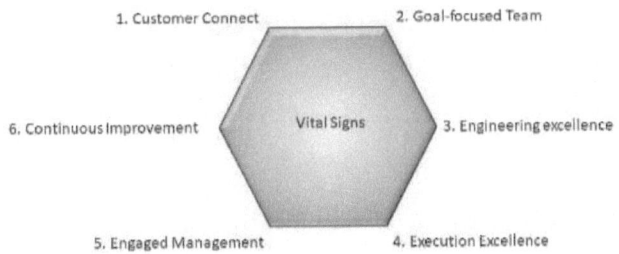

Introduction | 31

"No, it does not. It just gives us the vital signs, except for the example I quoted above. We will need to figure out the components and manifestations."

Arjuna asked, "How will we do that?"

Krishna thought for a while. "My idea is that you should use some of the projects within the Kurukshetra to understand the vital signs. You can talk to the project manager and team members to gather inputs. These raw inputs can be used to define the components and manifestations. Since you are new, you may not have had a chance to understand all the projects within the program well. These discussions with the projects will also serve to help you understand these projects well."

"That makes sense. Okay. I will come back to you with the raw information after I talk to each team. With your help, I can put together the method for defining that vital sign. How long do you think this exercise will take?"

Krishna said, "I was thinking of completing this exercise in a couple of weeks. Before you meet each project team, you should put together a set of points so that the discussions become easy. You will need separate sets of discussion points for different levels of team members."

Arjuna asked, "But, Krishna, the vital signs approach suggested by Ananth et al seems to focus mainly on traditional project development approach. While some of the important projects in my program are using the traditional approach, some projects are using the Agile approach. Will the vital signs developed for the traditional approach-based projects be valid for Agile projects? Will they be completely different? Or will they be essentially the same with some tweaks to accommodate the changed approach?"

Krishna said, "I think it will be the last. Let us not worry about Agile development approaches for now. Once we get the vital signs, components and manifestations for non-Agile project environments established, we can look at Agile projects."

"Okay. Understood. One thing, Krishna, once we have these vital signs, components and manifestations, how do we then assess a project?"

"Ah, this is where the inputs you received from Draupadi become important. Once we have the vital signs, components and manifestations, we can devise a survey, which can then be applied to stakeholders from different vantage points to get a 360-degree view of the status of each of these."

"How will that work?"

"We can elaborate on that later. First, let us get the vital signs, components and manifestations determined."

Krishna continued, "I also think that you should talk to Yudhishthira. He is wise and has a lot of experience. He can give you inputs on this. Also, talk to a few external consultants and project managers."

Arjuna said, "Okay. That makes sense."

Krishna said, "Come back to me after you have talked to the first team. What is the first vital sign you propose to tackle?"

"Customer Connect."

Krishna said, "Good choice. All the best for your discussions. And, Arjuna, one thing to remember is that with your exercise, we will be nailing down the vital signs of projects. Remember, however, that you are leading a program. At the end of the exercise, you may need to figure out some vital signs of a program to ensure that the program itself is healthy."

"Oh, yes. I hadn't thought of that."

"Don't worry about it now. Like the vital signs for Agile-based projects, we will look at this later or in a separate exercise."

Duryodhana and Shakuni

Duryodhana, the COO of Kaurava Software, sat in his office and gazed across the thoroughfare at the offices of Pandava Solutions. He was worried. Will his organization win against Pandava? He refused tea offered by his assistant.

He called in his Program Management Officer to his office. Shakuni, the PMO, was known as a wheeler-dealer. He was not known to be overly concerned about ethics in business dealings. He had organized to have one of the Pandava managers report to him about what was happening there.

Duryodhana said, "Shakuni, come in. Have a coffee or tea?"

Shakuni accepted the tea and sat down. He was a very experienced man, much older than Duryodhana.

"So, how are things going on with the Pandavas? And how are we doing?"

Shakuni considered, "They are doing well. However, we are much ahead of them in the development."

Duryodhana became worried, "What about quality? In our hurry to meet the deadline, are we sacrificing quality?"

"I don't think so. Well, not anything that will be noticed."

"What do you mean?"

Shakuni said, "We are making sure the product meets the stated quality requirement."

Duryodhana was worried about the "not anything to be noticed" bit let slip by Shakuni. But he did not pursue it with him.

"Anyway, what are the Pandavas up to?"

"They have a new program manager, Arjuna. He is very smart. I understand from my source, somebody in the program manager's office, that he and his coach Krishna have somehow got it into their heads that projects under this program and indeed this program itself should be 'healthy,' in addition to meeting the requirements."

Duryodhana was interested, "What is that? It sounds interesting."

Shakuni explained to Duryodhana the concept of the vital signs to assess the wellness of a project and also the 360-degree vantage point approach to assessing it.

"How are they looking at doing it?"

Shakuni said, "By continuously assessing the projects' health and making the needed improvements. They are developing a framework for assessing projects so that they have a holistic view of project health and an objective way to let the customer know what is happening and to get customer inputs; this also provides for a systematic approach for providing ongoing and timely guidance to the project managers and other managers."

Duryodhana asked, "What does that mean?"

Shakuni said, "The framework will give a view whether projects would not only deliver better products but also ensure that the ongoing development is healthy. A 'better system' meant not just the quality of the delivered product. It also meant the quality of the development practices."

Duryodhana asked, "I am worried. How will the customer view this? Will this not be the USP for the Pandavas? If they devise an instrument using which the customer can go in at any time and assess how healthy the project is, won't it put them one up on us? We won't have this kind of instrument."

He continued his train of thought. "Should we also be implementing something like the framework the Pandavas are implementing?"

Shakuni did not like this. He was worried that the control that he had through his office would be diluted. "No, we don't need anything new. We have processes in place to address all that."

Duryodhana asked, "But how will the customer react?"

Shakuni said, "What 'framework?' The customer will finally ask only a couple of questions. 'Is the constituent system done on time?;' 'Can we integrate it into the defense system and implement it now?;' 'Are there any bugs?' These are all. I think when we go back to the defense department with finished, working constituents before schedule, they will be happy to accept it. I don't think they will be coming to us during the development to check on the 'health.'"

"That is one of the conditions isn't it? That they can check on the quality of the development process?"

"It is. Our processes are CMMi and ISO compliant; we have regular quality audits by an independent function. That should be adequate."

"But, what if the Pandavas, once they have their instrument, trigger this idea with the customer?"

"We can talk to the customer and nix the idea."

Duryodhana changed tack, "But what about in the long run? Will not the customer realize that the Pandavas' success is repeatable while ours may not be? Will not the customer then turn on us?"

"What are you talking about? Our systems will be okay. If they detect some problems with it later on, surely, we would have all moved on? Remember, Duryodhana, in the long run we are all dead!"

Duryodhana said, "That is correct. But my other worry is if we do not address the process questions now, will we start finding problems as we near the delivery time?"

"No. Our processes are secure."

Chapter 2

Customer Connect
Contractual Commitments Management

Arjuna was feeling refreshed and energetic. He had completed a seven-kilometer run that morning. He did it in forty-two minutes. Six minutes a kilometer was not too bad!

He was happy with the ideas that he and Krishna had evolved about coming up with a framework for assessing project health. He knew that of all the vital signs, 'Customer Connect' had the primacy of importance.

To understand 'Customer Connect,' first of all, he had to understand the contract with the customer. He fixed a meeting with the Legal Manager of the program, Chitrangada.

Chitrangada was sitting in his office with two of his assistants. They were poring over some documents. Arjuna could see the "Whereas"-es and the "Inasmuch"-es all over the documents!

Chitrangada waved Arjuna in. "How can I help you? I have only half-an-hour. I have another meeting after this."

"Okay. I will be quick. And if need be, I can come back another day."

"Finish this off today. I may not have time after today."

Arjuna thought, "Oh! Such a busy man!" Aloud he said, "Okay. You know, I took over as the program manager of the Kurukshetra Program recently. The contracts with the customer were made before I came into this job. I understand that you are the person who worked on the customer contract for the program. I want to get an idea of the contract and the terms and how well we are implementing it."

"I don't know why you are so worried about this. I will take care of the contract. Leave it in my hands."

Arjuna would not give up, "As the program manager I want to ensure that we have the basics in place to eventually deliver a superior customer experience. So, I need to understand the contract well."

Chitrangada knew that he had met his match. He said, "Okay. What do you want to know?"

Arjuna asked, "How well have the terms of the contract been communicated to the project teams of the program?"

"Well, the project teams have been made aware of the terms of the statement of work. We thought it may not be necessary to keep them involved in other aspects of the contract, since their main job is to work on the delivery."

Arjuna was a bit concerned. But, he did not show it. He said, "For the team to deliver as per the contract, is it not important that they understand the terms of it? From your answer, I can infer that the team is not fully aware of this."

"We did not want to unnecessarily burden the project teams with mundane details of the contract. It may detract from their work if they worry about contract clauses."

Arjuna said, "There may be some clauses hidden in the contract that may mean some design considerations. For example, there could be, I am not saying there is, but there could be a requirement that forbids us from using open source software. If the project teams are not aware of this, they may end up being in violation of the contract."

Chitrangada appeared a bit nonplussed. "I had not thought of it that way."

Arjuna said, "Please make sure that the project teams have full access to the contract so the project manager can review it to see if there are some surprises."

"Okay. I will do that. Please talk to Yudhishthira to talk to my manager, the VP of legal, to ensure that I do not get into any trouble for making the contract public."

"It is not the public! It is just the project teams."

"Still."

"Okay. I will talk to Yudhishthira. If need be, any confidential aspects can be redacted."

Arjuna now knew one thing. The team was completely unaware of the terms of the contract. However, he wanted to verify this. So, he set up a meeting with Abhimanyu, the project manager of Chakravyuha, one of the component projects of Kurukshetra.

As mentioned before, Chakravyuha was one of the key constituent projects of Program Kurukshetra. The project involved developing and implementing a complex algorithm to provide a defensive net around Hastinapura. It was a key constituent of the defense system.

It was a large project with more than one hundred and fifty highly skilled engineers on it.

The project manager in charge of this project was Abhimanyu, one of the youngest project managers in Pandava. Arjuna had a good feeling about Abhimanyu. Of course, he was still learning, but he had an enthusiasm that bode well for the project. Abhimanyu was an expert on the implementation of complex algorithms for visual image processing for early warning systems. This was his second project as a project manager. He was also being coached by Krishna. For Arjuna, this was a great plus.

Arjuna's idea was that he could explore the "Customer Connect" vital sign with Abhimanyu and the team members and other stakeholders in detail so that he could distill out the manifestations that would help him continuously assess the state of the vital sign and improvement opportunities as the project progressed. This was why he had come to meet Abhimanyu.

"Abhi, I will not take too much of your time. Tell me how aware are you and your team members about the terms of the contract with the customer?"

"Very unaware! We are aware of the statement of work, but the other terms have not been discussed with me or the other team members. This is true not only of Chakravyuha, but also of the other projects within Kurukshetra."

Arjuna was now clear that the contract terms had remained within the citadels of the legal office.

Arjuna immediately went to Yudhishthira's office and apprised him of the situation with the contract. Yudhishthira was surprised.

He said, "What is the practice in place for contractual commitment management?"

Arjuna said, "There are no practices. The contract seems to be a separate animal from the project!"

Yudhishthira said, "Talk to Krishna, and work out the manifestations and the practices in this area. Using this, I can talk to the concerned VP to ensure that the project teams get adequate visibility of the contract."

Arjuna met Krishna the next day. He told Krishna about the brick wall he was hitting against with the legal office.

Krishna said, "We can work out the details of what is needed ourselves. Then, Yudhishthira can take it up at the appropriate levels."

Arjuna said, "Okay. I like the term used by Yudhishthira, 'contractual commitment management.' I think this can be the name of the component that encompasses the contract management aspects within the vital sign 'Customer Connect.'"

Krishna said, "Okay. This is a good term. Let us go with it. What are the manifestations and practices?"

Arjuna said, "The team has to clearly understand what the commitments are."

Krishna said, "Yes, there needs to be comprehensive training conducted so that the project teams clearly understand contractual commitments with counterpart/end customer and the consequences of not meeting them."

"Yes, that is exactly what is needed. This is where the legal office has to cooperate."

"Don't worry about their cooperation. I think Yudhishthira will ensure that."

Krishna continued, "As part of this training, it is also imperative that the documents related to the commitments are made available to the team."

"What kind of documents?"

"Service Level Agreements, Statement of Work, Master Service Agreement, etc."

"Okay. This is important. Right now, they are all considered as 'secret' documents by the legal office."

Krishna said, "Like the documents pertaining to the customer contract, all documents and details pertaining to any supplier contracts also should be available."

Arjuna said, "These documents can then be used, in addition to the training, to ensure that all commitments and operational performance clauses are clearly understood by the team. In fact, these may be needed to ensure that the product being developed is fully as per commitment."

"Exactly."

Krishna said, "It is easy to make commitments. But how do we know we are meeting the commitments?"

Arjuna said, "The project plans should be reviewed to ensure that contractual commitments have been considered."

Krishna asked, "For example?"

Arjuna said, "One of the clauses could be about whether there is a cap on the liability in case of software malfunction or the liability is unlimited. Another could be a clause on the non-use of open source software."

Krishna said, "We need to ensure that we do not actually infringe on these commitments."

Arjuna asked, "And if we do want to use a bit of open source software in the code, we need to get that authorized by the customer."

"Exactly. But, the question is why are we using this bit of open source software? Maybe it is because to meet some urgent customer need, it is easier to use the open source software than to develop the software ourselves, right? We need to ensure that either we conform to the letter of the contract or seek a deviation with approval from the customer."

Customer Connect | 45

Arjuna said, "Yes, I understand."

Krishna continued, "The next point is key. Remember, the key is that we should be a partner of the customer with a win-win relationship? We need to foster innovation in the team and make sure that the customer gets the benefit of that?"

"Yes?"

"In the same manner, we should be in a position to renegotiate commitments for mutual win, where possible, to enable long-term relationship with the customer."

"Like telling the customer, that in a particular situation, it is better to use open source software than developing solutions anew?"

"Absolutely."

Arjuna asked, "What else, Krishna?"

Krishna said, "This is it. These are the practices we need to have in place to ensure a good management of contractual commitment."

Arjuna said, "Okay, let me summarize:

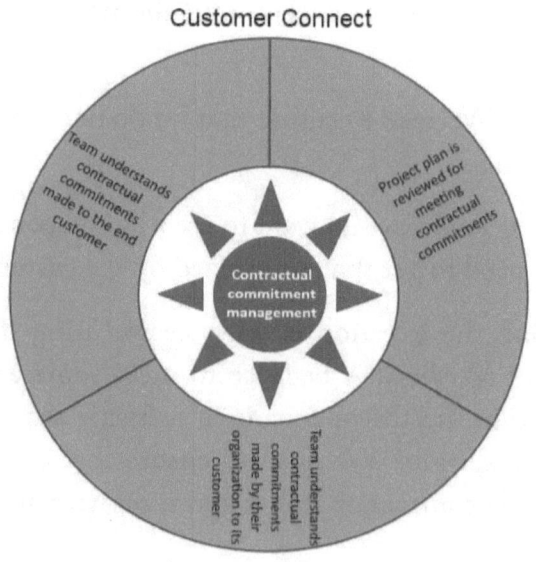

Component:

Contractual commitment management

Manifestations:

- Project team clearly understands contractual commitments with counterpart/end customer and the consequences of not meeting them.
- Project plan is reviewed for meeting contractual commitments.
- Commitments are re-negotiated for mutual win where possible, to enable long-term relationship between customer and other stakeholders."

"This is well summarized. Good going, Arjuna."

Rigor in Change Management

Sudas and Divodasa were program managers, like Arjuna, in other software companies. They had been colleagues in the same company when they started their careers. They had subsequently moved on to different organizations for career advancement.

Arjuna and Sudas were invited by Divodasa for a game of poker that evening at his house. Some other friends of Divodasa had also been invited. They had a few drinks and started the poker session in earnest. The stakes were low. The highest anyone could bet was ₹100.

The game went on, and the players were getting tipsy as they continued drinking. Arjuna remembered one hand very well. They had all placed an ante of ₹10 and received their first cards. Arjuna had drawn the 8, 7, 6 of hearts and the 5 of spades and the 4 of diamonds. Already a straight!

He did not want to let others know early on that he had a straight. So, he bet like the others without raising the stakes too much.

Then came the draw round. Why should he change his cards? He already had a straight and would do well. He was almost certain to win. But, what if somebody produced a flush?

He had drunk enough to take a chance. He changed two cards – the 5 of spades and the 4 of diamonds. And, what did he get as change cards?! The 5 and 4 of hearts! He had a straight flush!

He raised the stakes to the highest, and when the cards were put down, he realized that he did right to change his cards. One of the others had a king-high straight!

The next day, Arjuna had very detailed discussions with Abhimanyu and Krishna on the rigor of change management in project Chakravyuha.

Arjuna was thinking of his game of poker the previous night. He told them about this one deal where he made a decision to change two cards and how this change won him the deal.

Krishna said, "Yes, sometimes you have to embrace change. This will bring you rewards."

He continued, "The overall objective of each player is to make money. This objective is percolated down to each deal. The objective of each player in each deal is to make money. But while you are progressing toward that, there may be a need to change tack to maximize your benefits. There may be a risk you are taking with the change, but you have to weigh the benefits against the risks."

"I understand that good players have statistical rules innately built into their brains, ha, ha, to decide when to make changes."

Krishna said, "Yes. They have a comprehensive change management plan!"

He continued, "You will need to make a decision when there is an opportunity to change to maximize your benefits. Sometimes, if you miss the opportunity, the benefits may not be realizable. In the words of the immortal bard, 'There is a tide in the affairs of men, which taken at the flood, leads on to fortune…'"

Krishna asked Abhimanyu, "First of all, there needs to be a comprehensive and appropriate way of handling change. Does your project have this?"

"Yes."

"That's a good start. And do you know if change requests are captured formally?"

"Well, that is an issue. Sometimes, if the customer asks for a change, the development team 'just does it.'"

Krishna said, "Okay, so, sometimes the changes and their impact are not formally analyzed and discussed with the customer, right?"

"Yes, sometimes they are not."

"What about other stakeholders?"

"No."

"Are the changes to the requirements bubbled through all the different artifacts like functional documents and design documents and test plans?"

"I do not think so. These practices have to be rigorously enforced."

Krishna said, "Good, so, we have the manifestations of Rigor in Change Management. Arjuna can you summarize them?"

"OK. Here goes:

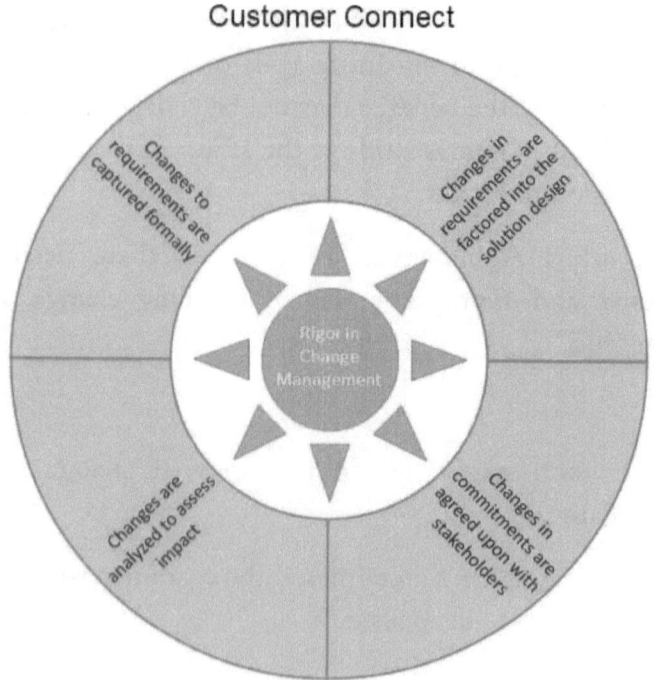

Component:

Rigor in Change Management

Manifestations:

- Changes to customer requirements for software are captured formally in a comprehensive manner.
- Impact of the changes is analyzed by the team, and possible scenarios for accommodating the changes are discussed with the customer to reach a common understanding and decisions.
- Changes in commitments and objectives and the resource requirements are discussed with all stakeholders to arrive at a consensus.
- Changes to requirements are factored into the solution design and implemented effectively to meet the revised commitments and objectives."

Krishna said, "Arjuna, do you realize that these manifestations, with some change of words, can apply equally to Agile projects?"

"Really?"

"Yes, anyway, let us not discuss that now. We can take it up later."

Krishna continued, "You know, Arjuna, the next key component of Customer Connect that you should look at is one of the most important."

"What is it?"

"This is an area where many organizations make a mess of things. It is Operational Connect with Customer."

"Of course, this is one of the key components."

Operational Connect with Customer

Arjuna was at the local pub near his apartment. His company, the Pandavas, were good paymasters, and Arjuna could afford to rent a good apartment near a green belt. Just outside the complex was a large mall where his family could buy all the necessities for their day-to-day lives. There was also a good watering hole nearby! Arjuna was quaffing beer with his buddies Sudas and Divodasa. They also lived in the same apartment complex that Arjuna lived in.

They talked about this and that and finally arrived at the topic that concerned all three of them most at the moment – program management.

Arjuna told them, without divulging anything confidential, about how he was trying to put together a set of parameters for assessing project health.

He said, "One of the key vital signs of a project is Customer Connect. I have arrived at a few components and manifestations of this vital sign. I can look at these to ensure that the project is ticking along healthily."

Sudas asked, "What are some of the components of Customer Connect?"

Arjuna said, "I have arrived at two already – Contractual Commitments Management and Rigor in Change Management."

Divodasa said, "These are correct parameters. What else are you looking at?"

Arjuna asked, "Can you fellas think of some of the other parameters one should look at?"

Sudas said, "Okay, you now have the lowest level of components for connect like contracts and change management. You should now start looking at getting these together with what you would do operationally with the customer. You know the day-to-day operational connect with the customer."

"What do you mean by that?"

"You know, things like project reports and the like, regular communications..."

Divodasa said, "Good. And things like release planning, escalations, etc."

Arjuna said, "This is starting to make sense. We need to ensure that the operational connect with the customer is healthy."

Arjuna was pleased that he was having this discussion. He already had one more component to look at and elaborate on.

He chewed on some French fries and said, "The next two rounds of beer are on me. I think I have gained a lot from this discussion. Did you listen to the new song by the Insects?"

"I find that they are crap. They are just trying to imitate the ancient group Beatles and doing a bad job at it."

"I thought they were OK…"

* * *

Arjuna knew that the area of operational connect with the customer was one which Abhimanyu, the project manager, would know well. This was something he should be doing on a regular basis.

"Abhi, one of the key areas of the vital sign Customer Connect is Operational Connect with Customer. What are the different aspects of this operational connect that you are familiar with? What are the practices you do in this area?"

Abhimanyu thought for a while. "Well, we are quite regular with our project reports. We send one weekly. We also send some overall status reports monthly and a technical report quarterly."

Arjuna said, "It is important that the operational connect is bi-directional. Do you have regular interactive calls with the customer where the customer representative would be able to communicate any business aspects in the context of the project so that relevant actions can be identified for both sides?"

"Yes. We understand that. We do have occasional formal calls."

"Does the customer get back to us on these reports that you send them?"

"Sometimes. Mainly if the reports are delayed."

"Do they ever come and ask us some questions about some aspect of the report?"

"No."

"Who do you send the reports to?"

"To the manager in charge of Chakravyuha."

"You mean your point of contact with the customer?"

"Yes."

Arjuna asked, "Do any of the team members send reports or talk to their counterparts about the status of the project?"

"No."

"What about escalations? Do you get any escalations from your customer?"

"Sometimes. What I do is call the team member concerned and ask her to fix the problem."

"How do you deal with the escalation call?"

"I tell the person who is escalating the issue to not worry. We will get the problem fixed."

Arjuna asked, "Are the team members involved in analyzing escalation and implementing preventive measures?"

"They are on an as-needed basis."

Arjuna continued, "When do you escalate a problem to me? How do you do it?"

"What do you mean?"

"What do you do if you cannot sort out an issue?"

"We try to sort out all issues."

Arjuna said, "I think we should put in place an escalation process. If you spend a particular amount of time on an issue and can't solve it, you should escalate it to me."

"You know, you are right. I never thought of it."

"Only then can you get management support for escalations."

"I understand."

Arjuna had to leave. He had a meeting fixed with Krishna. He said, "OK. Thanks. I will come back to you."

Arjuna went in search of Krishna.

"Do you have some time? I want to talk to you about Operational Connect with Customer."

"Okay. What is that?"

Arjuna said, "I had a drink with a couple of my friends. They are both program managers in large organizations. They suggested an area that can be a component of the vital sign Customer Connect – Operational Connect with Customer."

"Good. This area is one of the right ones to be a component of Customer Connect."

"I also met with Abhimanyu, the project manager of Chakravyuha. He gave me some interesting insights into what we are doing and what we are not in this component."

Krishna said, "One of the key manifestations of the operational connect with the customer is the sending of regular status reports at different levels. Is this happening?"

"To some extent, yes. The team is sending weekly, monthly and quarterly reports to the project point of contact. I also send project reports to my contact person."

Krishna asked, "The key thing is the customer response to these reports. Do they respond regularly or do they just file it away?"

"I think the latter."

Krishna said, "I think this is important. In addition to sending the report at different levels, customer's responses must be sought on these reports. This is what ensures for us that the customer clearly understands the status."

"Okay."

Krishna asked, "What about customer complaints?"

"I think they have a formal process for that. They receive the complaints that are registered, then analyze them and discuss them with the customer and resolve them. They track the complaint from registration to closure."

"How about escalations? How do they handle them?"

"There is no formal process or escalation path defined. It just somehow happens."

Krishna said, "This is important."

Krishna continued, "I think now we are in a position to put together the manifestations and practices of the component 'Operational Connect with Customer.'"

Arjuna said, "Okay. First, regular communication with the customer regarding operational status – weekly, monthly, quarterly – exists, and this includes channels for the customer to respond to the status reports."

"Good. What about communication at different levels?"

Arjuna said, "Yes. This is a manifestation."

Krishna asked, "What next?"

"The next one is having a formal process for escalation within the organization and escalations by the customer."

"What about preventive measures?"

"Yes. We need to ensure that in case of an escalation, whether internal or from the customer, there is a process for conducting a root cause analysis of the problem and putting in place preventive measures."

Krishna said, "That sounds good. Also, you mentioned another aspect that you had discussed with Abhimanyu?" Arjuna said, "Oh, yes. Management support for escalations."

Arjuna was satisfied. It looked like he had cracked the manifestations of the Operational Connect with Customer vital sign.

He summarized:

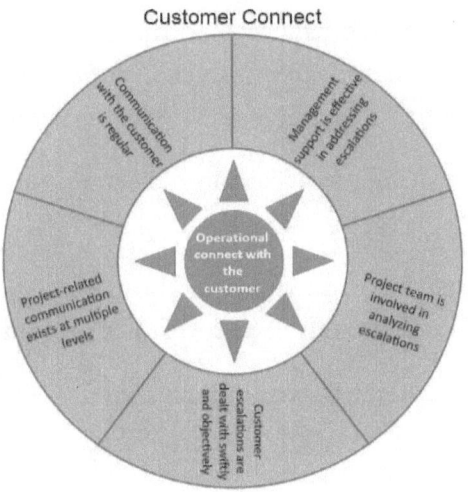

Component:

Operational connect with the customer

Manifestations:

- Regular communication with the customer exists regarding project status – weekly, monthly, quarterly.
- Project-related communication exists between project hierarchy and the customer at multiple levels.
- Customer escalations are dealt with swiftly and objectively, and preventive steps are taken to avoid recurrence.
- Project team is involved in analyzing escalations and implementing preventive actions for the future.
- Management support is effective in assisting/supporting project escalations."

Krishna said, "You have summarized this well. What is your next component?"

Arjuna said, "This is what I have been grappling with. I have been thinking…"

Krishna said, "You have been moving from the lowermost, in terms of relationship with customer, components to higher and higher ones. You now have covered Contractual Commitment Management, Rigor in Change Management and Operational Connect with Customer. I think the next component should be measuring how happy the customer is."

"You mean customer satisfaction measurement?"

"I mean *Actionable* Customer Satisfaction Measurement. Your measuring of customer satisfaction should be specific enough to be acted upon. It is useful only if you can act on your findings."

"Of course. I will get to work on this area."

Actionable Customer Satisfaction Measurement

Arjuna looked in the dictionary. It defined satisfaction as "the fulfillment of one's wishes, expectations, or needs, or the pleasure derived from this."

Arjuna knew enough about Indian philosophy to know that satisfaction, or for that matter dissatisfaction, is not permanent. Where satisfaction comes from things you can't control, you know that it cannot be permanent.

Of course, Arjuna knew that he could not satisfy the customer with this philosophy! He needed to make sure that the customer was always satisfied. He needed to measure customer satisfaction levels and take actions to remove any dissatisfaction.

The next morning, Arjuna met Abhimanyu in the Pandava cafeteria. Abhimanyu ordered a glass of milk and pancakes with lots of butter, while Arjuna had toast and omelet and a cup of coffee.

Arjuna spread butter on his toast and asked, "What do you understand by customer satisfaction?"

Abhimanyu thought. "Well, as far as I can see, it is a measurement of how our project's outputs are meeting and exceeding the customer's expectations."

"Perfect. You have understood this concept well. Now, tell me, why do we need to measure customer satisfaction?"

"To clearly understand whether the customer is happy with our product or not. It gives a vehicle for the customer to give his opinions. It therefore reduces uninformed negative talk by the customer."

"Excellent. Yes, it is important that we provide a vehicle through which the customer can express any dissatisfaction. Why else?"

"It provides an early indicator of whether we will retain this customer for newer orders."

"Right again. How do you measure customer satisfaction?"

"We can do surveys through formal mechanisms; we can look at what customers say about us in the different media including social media. We should also get inputs at various levels. We can form special groups with the customer included and see what inputs are got in these meetings. For example, we can have a group focused on development approaches. When this group meets, they can ask for customer inputs."

Arjuna said, "Okay, Abhi, let us take your project. When do you measure customer satisfaction?"

"We do it once a month. We think this is enough."

"Yes. This should be enough."

"What kind of things do you measure to understand customer satisfaction?"

"We send around a questionnaire asking the customer if they are satisfied or not. That is it."

"Okay. I think you need to measure multiple dimensions of customer satisfaction."

"For example?"

"For example, efficiency of deliverables, project performance, relationship strength, team capability, transactional effectiveness, etc."

"Okay, we do most of these."

Arjuna asked, "What do you do when you get this input from the customer?"

Abhimanyu looked sheepish. "Pretty much nothing. We do not really know how to respond to the survey result."

Arjuna said, "I think this is where we need to be careful. The customer's input often carries hints of things going wrong. Often managers say things like *'customer says this but the project reality is different; I just need to educate the customer on the reality; no other actions are required.'* I cannot stress enough the golden rule that 'customer perception is reality.' This will help to drive necessary actions."

Abhimanyu looked positively guilty.

Arjuna continued, "And, this is where the multi-dimensional satisfaction measurements also will help. Unlike with an overall response, you can analyze the inputs received and identify improvement actions that have measurable impact on project performance."

"Okay, this makes sense."

Arjuna said, "You talked of some formal mechanisms to get satisfaction inputs from the customer. Do you have any informal mechanisms?

For example, when you or a team member talks to a customer, do you sense her satisfaction levels?"

"Yes. We sometimes can get a feel for the customer's satisfaction in this informal manner."

Later in the day, Arjuna met Krishna and apprised him of the inputs he had received from Abhimanyu.

Krishna asked, "What should the manifestations of Actionable Customer Satisfaction Measurement be?"

Arjuna said, "Let me try to summarize what I derived from my discussion with Abhimanyu:

Component:

Actionable customer satisfaction measurement

Manifestations:

- Customer satisfaction is measured to provide insights on customer perception of performance at appropriate intervals and checkpoints.
- Multiple dimensions of customer and user satisfaction are measured; e.g. efficiency of deliverables, project performance, relationship strength, team capability, transactional effectiveness.
- Customer satisfaction data is analyzed to identify improvement actions that have measurable impact on project performance.
- Project team seeks customer feedback on an ongoing basis during the project.
- Customer satisfaction is also sensed through inter-personal interactions between the customer and project team."

Krishna said, "This is great. You have captured this well. Let us go with this."

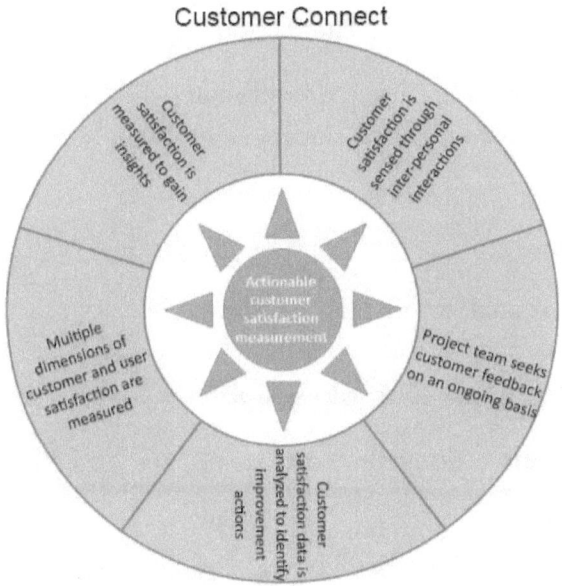

He continued, "You know, Arjuna, when I used to work as project manager, I had a simple technique to get a basic understanding of whether customer satisfaction is growing or declining."

"What was this technique?"

"I did what you can call a sentiment analysis on key emails from any customer."

"How did you do that?"

"Keep a dictionary of 'good' words and phrases and 'bad' words and phrases. For example, 'happy' is a good word, 'unhappy' is a bad word. 'Problem' is a bad word. 'Thank you' is a good phrase, etc."

Krishna continued, "The idea is to search all the mails from a particular customer and see the trend. Does it go from more 'good' words to less? Has the number of 'bad' words increased recently? All these give the trend of a particular customer's satisfaction level at various points in time. Of course, these then need to be validated during customer interactions. But, these trends from emails can help you proactively address customer satisfaction issues."

"This is a good idea. We can automate this trend analysis system. This will make it easy to read the customer's mails to various people in the project."

"Good idea."

Arjuna went back to his office, upbeat.

Product and Business Domain Insight

Arjuna was walking along the corridors of his office building, deep in thought.

"Penny for your thoughts." It was Priyamvada. She worked in the program business office.

He said, "Nice to see you, Priyamvada. I was thinking about the vital signs of my projects. I am trying to put in place the components of one key vital sign, 'Customer Connect.'"

Priyamvada said, "You know, Arjuna, I have always felt that one of the key ways to connect to the customer is through good knowledge of the business and the product domain. This will help your interactions with the customer go smoothly and also help you identify opportunities to add value to the customer."

She smiled at him and went her way.

One of the worries that Arjuna always had was whether his project team members had knowledge of the domain of their projects. And, what was the customer's reason for developing this product at all.

In short, how good was the product and business domain insight of the members of his project teams.

Priyamvada's articulating precisely this got Arjuna thinking. Yes, product and business domain insight was a key component of the Customer Connect vital sign.

He decided to go back to the project Chakravyuha to get inputs on this area.

Arjuna decided to start with one of the module leaders, Uttara. He was a key person in the development and design of the algorithm.

He was a smartly dressed youngster in jeans and a T-shirt. He had headphones over his ears and was listening to some music (thought Arjuna).

Arjuna waved at Uttara. "Hello, Uttara. How are you?"

"Good. I heard you wanted to talk to me about my project. Is this some assessment of my performance?"

"No, no! Kurukshetra is a very key program for the Pandavas. It is imperative that we succeed. I am trying to figure out, with the help of Krishna, how we can assess the health on an ongoing project. This has nothing to do with individual performances. In fact, I am here to get inputs from you."

Uttara seemed to have been reassured of Arjuna's noble intentions and was ready to cooperate with him.

Arjuna asked, "What is your role in the Chakravyuha project?"

"My role is providing the leadership for ongoing design of the algorithms for drone control."

"Oh! That is an important role. Your drones are part of the surveillance set up, I suppose. They would, as they fly around, so to speak, detect possible threats to the city? You must be an expert in the area of controls to be able to design the algorithm for this?"

Uttara said, "No. I can't say I am an expert. I know enough to get by, I think. You know, I am a pure module leader. I think getting too technically involved or having deep knowledge of the domain may detract from my module leadership tasks."

Arjuna was surprised. "How?"

"I may start interfering in the technical areas and overlook my overall guidance work."

"But then who is the domain expert?"

"There is no expert as such. But most of the people in my team are good. They understand what the area is all about."

Arjuna asked, "When you say 'they understand the area,' what do you mean?"

"They are able to understand what the customer says so that the team can code and develop the product."

"Is that enough?"

"What more do we need? Our job is to develop the product as per the requirements of the customer."

Arjuna asked, "How will we know if the product is the best that the customer can get?"

"What do you mean? We do not pass any judgment on the product requirement per se. We just do what we are asked to do. Is that not what a vendor like us is supposed to do?"

Arjuna asked, "Does not the customer have an expectation that we will advise them on how to make the product better in terms of technology and competitiveness? After all, we are the consultants, aren't we?"

Uttara did not seem to understand this. He was intent on insisting that they were doing their job.

Arjuna tried to elaborate on his point. "Let us say that your drones detect something untoward. And the systems conclude that the city is under attack and sound warning sirens. But very soon you realize that it is false positive. There is no real danger. You then have to correct the threat perception, created by the sirens, among the citizens. The customer may not have explicitly stated this in his requirements. But as experts, don't we have to provide for this nonetheless?"

He continued, "My point is that as experts we should be able to identify unstated needs."

Uttara was even more confused. "If such an item, that is, recovery from false positives, is not stated in the requirements, the customer is not going to get it."

Krishna was amused when he saw Arjuna the next day. "When you went away after our meeting last time, you were upbeat. What happened between then and now?"

Arjuna said, "Well, Krishna, my despondency seems to come in cycles. I had a discussion with a module leader of Chakravyuha today. Things look pretty grim."

"What is the problem?"

Arjuna said, "Well, the team developing the Chakravyuha algorithms seems to have no knowledge of the domain at all. They have no sense of the product they are developing either. They just seem to be doing whatever, even if wrong, the customer is telling them to do. There is really no feedback from our team to the customer."

"You think this is not healthy?"

"Obviously not."

"Why?"

"What kind of Customer Connect do we have if the interactions with the customer cannot be two-way? Does not the customer expect us to give him feedback on the product and the domain?"

"Yes. The customer hired the Pandavas ostensibly on the basis of their superior knowledge of the domain!"

Arjuna said, "I am sure this is what the sales people would have told the customer."

"Ah."

Arjuna continued. "I think we need to make what the sales people told the customer true. We need to go all out to enhance our product and business domain insight."

"Good. So, you feel that one of the key components of 'Customer Connect' is 'product and business domain insight?'"

"Yes."

"And what are the manifestations of this component?"

"Well, I think there are four manifestations. They are:

Team has acquired the required level of product and business domain knowledge.

Team demonstrates product and domain knowledge through timely identification of unstated needs.

Team has the required opportunities to develop their product and business domain knowledge (e.g. training, industry forums and seminars).

Customer recognizes our team's ability to provide product & business domain insights."

Krishna said, "So these are the three manifestations?"

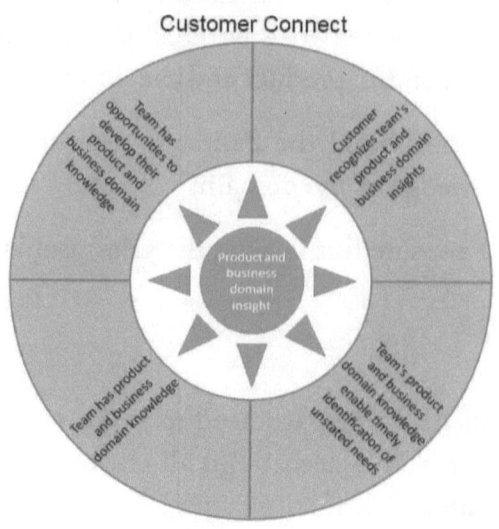

"Yes."

"And you are saying that we can assess the health of the project in the area of 'product and business domain insight' if we gauged the success of these three manifestations?"

"Yes."

"Good. I think we are getting somewhere."

Krishna continued, "Now I think we can come to the 'mother of all components' of 'Customer Connect .'"

"What is that?"

"Partnership with customer."

Partnership with Customer

Yudhishthira arranged for a meeting with Air Marshal Bharata, the program manager of Kurukshetra in the defense department. On the appointed day, Arjuna and Yudhishthira set out for Bharata's office in a busy corner of the department of defense offices. Well-turned out officers and soldiers were busily walking around, working on various tasks. Arjuna was surprised to see that there was not much saluting. He had somehow thought that all military officers always saluted each other! He seemed to be wrong.

They were welcomed by the aide-de-camp of the Air Marshal and taken to his office. They were offered juice, coffee and biscuits. Soon the Air Marshal Bharata walked in and was introduced to the Pandava people.

He was a simple looking man, and he politely greeted them, "Gentlemen."

Yudhishthira said, "It is our pleasure, Sir. We are happy that you could make time for us."

"I am always here to answer any question on the project. However, there is one condition. My assistant will note down any question you ask and the answers I give to them. Whatever answers I give you will be summarized and sent to the Kauravas also. We require to do this as part of our transparency policy."

Yudhishthira agreed to this condition. He then gave Bharata a ten-minute summary of the progress of the program. He then asked Arjuna to take over.

Arjuna fidgeted a little and said, "Sir, I will be quite honest with you. While the program is going okay, in our opinion, I have some concerns about execution practices. We want to ensure that whatever we do, we must meet the required quality and timeliness. But we must also follow the best possible practices so that we are able to deliver you something that is over and above what you have asked for."

"What do you mean by that?"

"For example, your requirements indicate that we use a particular type of technology for implementing a very important feature of the product. And certainly, we can do that. However, we feel that there is a better technology available for implementing this feature on. If this is used, we feel that the product will be much better in the long run."

"Okay. Go on."

"I find that in our scheme of things, we do not have any approach to bring up such suggestions to your team. Of course, investigating, understanding and implementing this technology makes for bigger investment of time and people power. But, it is certainly worth the investigation."

The Air Marshal said, "I am happy you brought it up. This is the kind of innovative ideas that I am looking for from developers like you. If you suggest a process, we will be happy to look at this. We are looking for partners, not just contractors."

He continued, "Look, there is a meeting of our technology review board coming up next week. I can send you an invitation to attend. You can put forward your ideas for this change and any other changes you think will make sense. Of course, for providing a level playing field, I will have to invite your competitor also."

Arjuna said, "Sir, would you like to meet some of our team members? I would like to invite you one day to our office to meet a project team and talk to them. Maybe at one of their retrospective sessions?"

"Certainly, I shall be delighted." He asked his assistant to make a note of this and fix a date.

Arjuna's head was in a swirl about how quickly the Air Marshal was responding to his suggestions.

When Arjuna reported on this conversation to Krishna later, he said, "And if your presentation to the technology review board goes well next week, we can suggest that our attending the review board meeting, if not every week, at least once a month, should be codified as part of the engagement."

Arjuna learned early on in his career that it was vital to understand the raison d'être for the project from the customer's point of view. For this, first he needed to talk to the sales manager who sold this program to the customer and Pandava's account manager for Kurukshetra.

He requested a conference call with these three. The call with the sales manager, Amba, and the account manager, Ambalika, took place on one of the evenings of that week.

It was after office time, and Arjuna had just got a call from his wife who was traveling on business that their live-in nanny had called saying that their five-year-old son had fallen down while playing and had hurt his knee.

He wanted to rush home when he realized that he had the con-call fixed. So, he called home and spoke to his son, comforted him and told him that he would be home soon.

He then went to the meeting room to take the con-call. He had also called in his admin assistant to take notes.

Arjuna started the discussion. "Ladies, you know that I have taken over as the program manager of Kurukshetra. This is a long program, and I want to ensure that we have a framework in place to continuously assess the health of the program and the component projects of the program."

He gave them a brief summary of his discussion with Air Marshal Bharata.

He continued, "I want to start by understanding how well we are connected to the customer at individual project levels first. Let us use the project Chakravyuha as a starting point for this. I would like you to tell me how well we are doing in this aspect on this project."

Ambalika, the account manager, said, "Yes, I have been meaning to talk to you. The customer, though generally happy with the project Chakravyuha, has lately been showing some dissatisfaction with the project. Note, although, that all the project metrics and progress measurements are green."

"I see, continue."

"Neither they nor I am able to put a finger on the problem, but I can see that the dissatisfaction is there."

Arjuna asked, "How good is our relationship with the customer..."

Amba, the sales manager, interrupted, "You probably know that our winning this project was based on our projection of our expertise, specifically, in the domain of defense shields. It is important that we live up to that claim and 'brand,' as it were. This will be the stepping stone for getting the customer to eventually treat us as a partner."

Customer Connect | 75

Arjuna asked, "Are you saying that the customer is yet not able to call us a partner in their business?"

"Exactly. We have some ways to go, including living up to our brand, before they would call us their partner."

Arjuna said, "I think we need to find ways to emphatically demonstrate to the customer that this is a win-win relationship."

Arjuna made a mental note to himself to go back to the Chakravyuha project team and stress the importance of living up to the customer's expectations of the brand that was sold to them.

Amba said, "Ambalika, you are the account manager. What are we doing in this aspect?"

Ambalika said, "I am trying to do two things. First of all, I am trying to make sure that the customer appreciates the benefit of this partnership. This is where we need support from you, Arjuna. You have to show us that we are doing well. Then we can get them to publicly acknowledge the benefits of the partnership."

She continued, "I am also trying to make sure that multiple layers in our hierarchy maintain relationships with appropriate levels in their hierarchy. In fact, recently I arranged for a call of our CEO with theirs. We want to aim for a 'broad-band connection' as opposed to a 'narrow-band connection.'"

"That is good. I think our meeting with the Air Marshal, which Yudhishthira also attended, was one of these at an organizational level."

He told them how he had been invited to attend the technology review board. "We can bring up some of our technology ideas at this meeting."

Arjuna then asked, "You know that I am new in the program. Is there a common engagement vision that is the foundation of this partnership?"

Ambalika said, "We, along with the customer, worked on a vision exercise at the beginning of the program. We also worked out strategies to realize this engagement vision. And we update each other as situations change. This overall program engagement vision has been percolated down to the projects – projects like Chakravyuha."

She pointed at Arjuna and said, "Arjuna, the project team should possess the ability to realize this vision in the project. This is a job for you."

Arjuna said, "Yes. I am working with Abhimanyu on this."

Ambalika said, "And, I think that it is on all of us to ensure that we make visible progress on realizing this common engagement vision. This also needs monitoring. I suppose this is something that Arjuna and Abhimanyu would be doing?"

"Yes. In fact, this call is part of that monitoring!"

"Of course."

Arjuna said, "Well, ladies, thank you for your time. I will update Yudhishthira about our discussions."

When Arjuna met Krishna next, Krishna said, "Arjuna, you look happy today. How were your discussions with the sales and account managers of Kurukshetra? From your comportment, I guess it went well?"

Arjuna said, "This went very well. These people are doing something. We took the project Chakravyuha and analyzed the Customer Connect of this project, especially the partnership aspect."

"Did you get the feeling that the customer considers the Pandavas as a partner with whom they can go to the next level of business?"

Arjuna thought, "Ah, not yet. We have some ways to go before that happens."

"How then did you get the feeling that they are doing a good job?"

"Well, first of all, there is a common engagement vision that exists for the program. This can form the foundation for partnership with the customer. This vision has been percolated down to all the projects including Chakravyuha."

"Do we have a planned, strategic approach to realize this engagement vision for Chakravyuha? I am assuming that if this engagement vision realization is successful in Chakravyuha, it should be so in other projects also."

"I think so. We have this. Of course, we should enable the teams to realize this."

Krishna asked, "But, do the teams possess the ability to realize this engagement vision over time?"

Arjuna said, "Yes. I think the Chakravyuha team does. It needs good leadership though."

"Ah. And, that is where you come in."

"Exactly. You hit it on the head."

Krishna continued, "Clearly, it is important that the customer should see Pandava as a partner with a mutual win-win relationship."

"I agree."

Krishna said, "Arjuna, for this to be successful, these engagements with the customer need to happen at different levels of the hierarchy to ensure validated inputs."

"Yes. This is important. These engagements should happen at different levels of the organization."

Krishna continued, "And, of course, there needs to be visible progress in the project to realize this vision and promote partnership. Otherwise, this vision will remain exactly that, a vision."

Arjuna asked, "Don't we need to ensure that people know that this partnership is progressing successfully?"

Krishna said, "Yes. We need to ensure that partnership benefits are realized and acknowledged publicly. Otherwise, the benefits of the partnership will not materialize."

Krishna continued, "This whole area of partnership with customer is often met with skepticism among project managers who are fighting to keep the project going on the ground!"

Arjuna asked, "Is it not true that this kind of relationship happens over time and over multiple projects?"

"True. It is however an aspirational goal – particularly for large, critical engagements. In fact, in such large programs as Kurukshetra, this is a required goal."

"That is right."

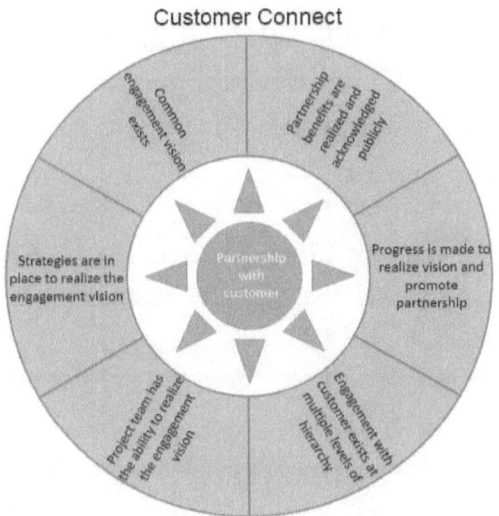

Krishna continued, "These, therefore, are the manifestations of the component 'Partnership with customer;' do you agree?"

Arjuna was happy, "Yes, I think that these are it. Let me summarize:

Component:

Partnership with customer

Manifestations:

- Common engagement vision exists as the foundation for partnership.
- Agreed strategies are in place to realize the engagement vision.
- Project team possesses the ability to realize the engagement vision over time.
- Engagement with customer exists at multiple levels of hierarchy to enable partnership.
- Visible progress is made in the project to realize vision/promote partnership.
- Partnership benefits are realized and acknowledged publicly."

"This is perfect. Well put."

Krishna continued, "Well, Arjuna. I think you have explained and codified the 'Customer Connect' vital sign pretty well. You are making good progress. What vital sign are you going to tackle next?"

"Well…"

Krishna said, "Why not Goal-Focused Team? After the customer, the most important stakeholder is the team. Let us take up Goal-Focused Team next."

Summing up Customer Connect

Before going on to the next vital sign, Goal-Focused Team, Krishna and Arjuna presented a summarized version of the components and manifestations of Customer Connect to Yudhishthira.

Yudhishthira asked, "Are these components and manifestations invariant across organizations and across methodologies and approaches?"

Krishna said, "Well, the vital signs and the components are more or less invariant. The manifestations may, however, vary across methodologies and approaches and different situations of projects."

Components	Manifestations
Contractual Commitment Management	The team clearly understands contractual commitments made to the end customer and the consequences of not meeting them
	The team understands contractual commitments made by their organization to its customer
	Project plan is reviewed for meeting contractual commitments

Components	Manifestations
Rigor in Change Management	Changes to customer requirements are captured formally in a comprehensive manner
	Impact of changes is analysed by the team and possible scenarios for accommodating the changes are discussed with the customer to reach a common understanding and decisions
	Changes in commitments and objectives and the resource requirements are discussed with all stakeholders to arrive at a consensus
	Changes in requirements are factored into the solution design and implemented effectively to meet the revised commitments and objectives
Operational Connect with Customer	Regular communication with the customer exists regarding project status – weekly, monthly, quarterly
	Project-related communication exists between project hierarchy and the customer at multiple levels
	Customer escalations are dealt with swiftly and objectively, and preventive steps are taken to avoid recurrence
	The team is involved in analyzing escalations and implementing preventive actions for the future
	Management support is effective in assisting/ supporting project escalations

Components	Manifestations
Actionable Customer Satisfaction Measurement	Customer satisfaction is measured to gain insight to customer perception of performance at appropriate intervals and checkpoints
	Multiple dimensions of customer and user satisfaction are measured: e.g., efficacy of deliverables, project performance, relationship strength, team capability, transactional effectiveness
	Customer satisfaction data is analyzed to identify improvement actions that have measurable impact on project performance
	The team seeks customer feedback on an ongoing basis during the project
	Customer satisfaction is also sensed through inter-personal interactions between the customer and the team
Product and Business Domain insight	Team has the required opportunities to develop their product and business domain knowledge
	Team has acquired the required level of product and business domain knowledge
	Team demonstrates product and domain knowledge through timely identification of unstated needs
	Customer recognizes our team's ability to provide product & business domain insights

Components	Manifestations
Partnership with Customer	Common engagement vision exists as the foundation for partnership
	Agreed strategies are in place to realize the engagement vision
	The team possesses the ability to realize the engagement vision over time
	Engagement with the customer exists at multiple levels of hierarchy to enable partnership
	Visible progress is made in the project to realize vision/promote partnership
	Partnership benefits are realized and acknowledged publicly

Chapter 3
Goal Focused Team

Arjuna's brother was an avid footballer. He was watching a replay of a match of the 2006 Football World Cup – Argentina vs Serbia & Montenegro. When Arjuna sat down with a beer next to his brother, what he saw mesmerized him. He was just in time to see the second goal by Argentina in their 6–0 drubbing of Serbia & Montenegro. It was a masterpiece!

Argentina quietly went through 21 passes, and then Riquelme fed Saviola who sent a pass inside for Cambiasso. Cambiasso passed the ball onto Crespo, who kicked a return pass with the back of his heel to Cambiasso, who then rammed the ball home from 12 yards.

When Arjuna met Krishna the next morning, he waxed eloquently to him about the 24-pass goal.

He said, "Argentina's focus on scoring the goal was complete. Nobody tried a long shot. Nobody tried to run with the ball. It was total and complete focus on one thing – the goal."

Krishna said, "Have you realized that this is exactly what is needed for projects also? A completely Goal-Focused Team? This is the second vital sign that gives the status of the overall health of the project."

Arjuna reacted as if he had attained enlightenment. "Wow! This is a great discovery. Yes, indeed. A Goal-Focused Team is key to the success of a project."

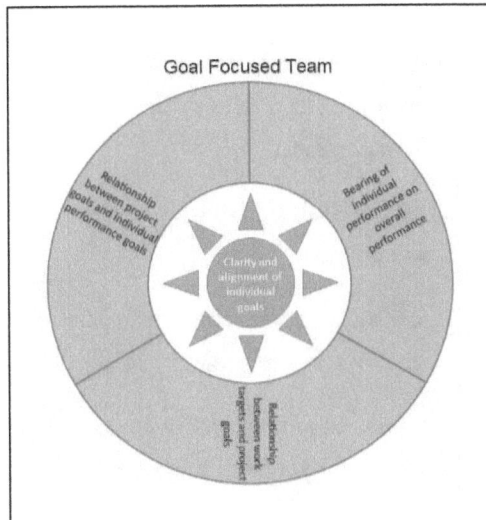

	Relationship between project goals and individual performance goals is discussed and agreed up front
	Relationship between work targets and project goals is well-understood
	Individual project performance has a significant bearing on overall performance

Krishna said, "First of all, you will note that there is a clear alignment of individual objectives and team objectives. No unnecessary shooting. Pass the ball to the person who has the best chance to score a goal. A player's objective is to perform as a team machine."

Arjuna said, "Similarly, there needs to be alignment between project goals and each team member's goals."

"Yes. And these need to be discussed and agreed upon upfront between management and the team member."

Arjuna said, "And, of course, the relationship between an individual's performance and the team's goals need to be clear."

"Right. If you watch the Argentinian team, you know that each player knows how his performance has a bearing on the overall team's performance. And, they know team success is a pre-requisite for individual success."

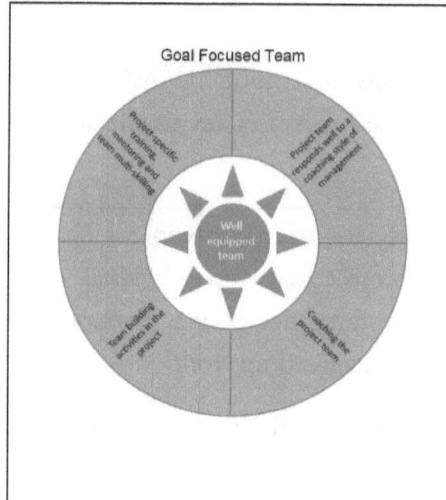

	Provision of project-specific training and support for skill development and multi-skilling of team members
	Provision of project-specific training & support for skill development of the Project Manager/Leads
	Team building activities in the project
	Coaching/mentoring of the project team to achieve project goals
	Project team responds well to a coaching style of management

Krishna said, "Of course, Arjuna, you realize that this team's performance on the field is no lucky fluke. They are a well-trained, well-equipped team."

"That is clear. They go through a rigorous training regime for development of each individual's specific skills. One may be a defender, one may be a forward, one may be a midfielder. Specific training is given for each role and skill."

Krishna said, "At the same time, team members need to be multi-skilled. Training should focus on this too. A defensive player should be skilled enough to take the ball to the goal and score if the right opportunity presents itself."

He continued, "They go through hundreds of simulated situations and know how to react in each situation. Team building activities form a core of their training regime."

"What about the coaches? They have a set of coaches who mentor and train the team to achieve great levels of football."

Krishna said, "Right, while not all of us can be a coach like José Pékerman, even in our project teams we need to bring in this concept of coaching individuals and the team to achieve project goals."

He continued, "And the key thing is that the team and the individuals should be able to thrive in a coaching style of management."

Arjuna agreed.

Krishna thought for a while and said, "The next important thing is teamwork. You saw how teamwork helped Argentina score this fabulous goal."

Arjuna said, "And this team work is a key thing for projects to attain their goals."

"Yes. Now, while we learn from the Argentinian team how to create a Goal-Focused Team, let us also look at some of the negative situations."

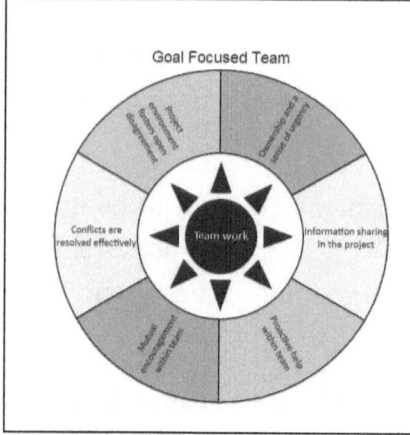

Project environment fosters open disagreement

Conflicts are resolved effectively

Mutual encouragement within team

Proactive assistance within team

Information sharing in the project

Ownership and sense of urgency

"What is that?"

"You know that in 2009, Riquelme quit from the Argentinian national team due to disagreements with Maradona."

Arjuna asked, "You are saying that a good project team will foster open disagreement? So, rash acts become unnecessary?"

"Exactly. And conflicts are quickly and effectively solved without any rancor."

Arjuna said, "And, on the other side, I suppose there needs to be mutual encouragement within the team?"

"Certainly. And proactive assistance. Each team member or player must come to the aid of the others in trouble. If a player is stuck between two good defenders, another player should be able to draw the defenders away. And, if a developer is stuck with a bug in a piece of code, another team member should rush to help him out."

Krishna continued, "Another key thing is information sharing. If a player finds out that an opposing player is weak in a particular situation on a particular day, this information needs to be shared with the rest of the team immediately so that the whole team can exploit this weakness. In the same way, information that is relevant to a project must be widely distributed within the project team."

Arjuna said, "Yes. And I suppose that none of these things will work if the team and players do not have a keen sense of ownership and urgency."

"Right."

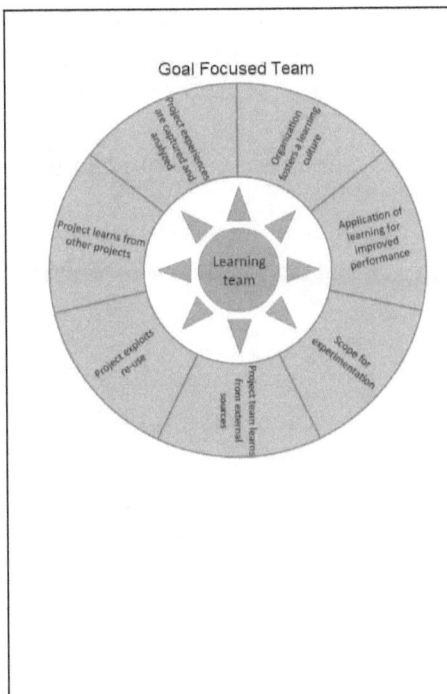

	Project experiences are captured and analyzed to identify lessons learned
	Project learns from other projects and shares learning with other projects
	Project exploits re-use
	Project learns from sources external to the organization
	Scope for experimentation
	Application of learning for improved performance (efficiency & effectiveness in achieving project goals)
	Organization fosters a learning culture

Krishna and Arjuna walked to the cafeteria for a cup of coffee.

Krishna asked, "What is the next takeaway from watching the Argentinian game of 2006?"

Arjuna said, "Team learning. I suppose Argentina learned from their 2002 World Cup debacle, when they lost to England and drew with Sweden in the play-offs and was knocked out of the tournament. I think they learned a lesson from this loss."

Krishna said, "Great. Good observation. I think similarly a project team should be able to learn as they go forward – from past mistakes, from past successes, from other projects' mistakes and successes."

Arjuna said, "Yes. These experiences must be captured and analyzed to identify what is to be learned."

Krishna said, "Correct. Another thing. One of the most damaging things I see in projects is the propensity to re-invent the wheel. A project manager or a team member needs to be able to re-use what is available. Many team members feel that they can do a better job starting afresh than if they re-use what is available."

Arjuna asked, "You are saying that we need what is equivalent to egoless programming?"

"Yes. Exactly. And note that learning is not just to learn new skills. Learning is also to improve one's performance."

"Yes. I remember how the Fosbury Flop revolutionized the sport of high-jump. The Fosbury Flop was necessary to improve a high-jumper's performance."

"Exactly. But, the key thing to remember is that along with learning, the environment must allow for experimentation and failures. Otherwise, no one will come up with new ideas."

"That is right."

Krishna said, "And, clearly, all this will not work if the organization, whether a football team or a software organization, does not foster a learning environment."

They ordered another coffee each.

Krishna said, "Argentina's 2002 World Cup debacle was clearly due to lack of motivation. They had a good coach, Marcelo Bielsa. They had a good team with quality players like Walter Samuel, Pablo Aimar, Juan Sorin and others. They were one of the favorites. But, what happened?"

Arjuna said, "While individual motivation was clearly there, team motivation must have been lacking."

"Yes. Both are needed to make a successful team. Similarly, in a software project, we need to ensure that there is motivation at both the individual level and in the project context."

Arjuna asked, "How does one apply this in the software project environment?"

"The coach of a football team or the project manager of a project should understand individual differences in motivation and take steps to address these individual motivational factors."

Arjuna said, "One of the things that I learned was that motivation levels increase when you have a clear idea of your career path, when you know you are making progress and when your project manager and the organization facilitates your career path and progression."

"Absolutely. And people should have the desire to be successful, whatever the hurdles in their way. I am reminded of footballer Styliyan Petrov of Bulgaria who overcame acute leukemia and went through painful sessions of chemotherapy and still managed to stage a comeback."

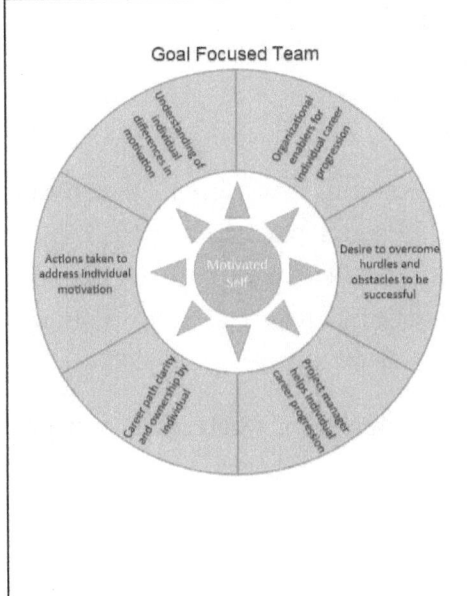

Understanding of individual differences in motivation

Actions are taken to address factors for individual motivation

Clarity of career path and ownership by individual

Facilitation of project manager for individual career progression

The desire to overcome hurdles and obstacles to be successful

Effective organizational enablers exist for individual career progression

Goal Focused Team | 93

Arjuna asked, "What about motivation in the team context?"

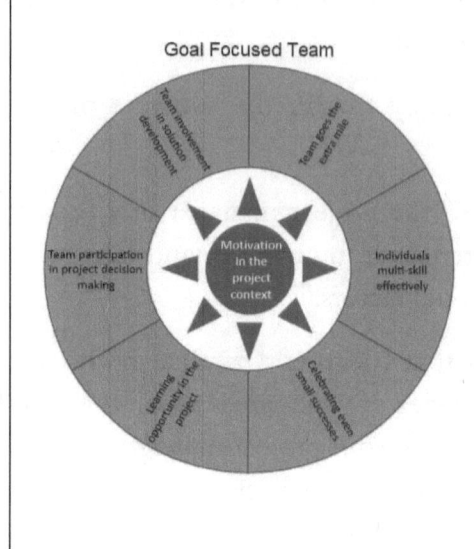

- Team involvement in solution development/validation
- Individuals multi-skill effectively to meet commitments
- Learning opportunity in the project for individuals
- Individuals go the extra mile to meet commitments
- The team goes the extra mile to meet commitments
- Celebrating even small successes
- Team participation in project decision making

"This can come when each member of the team feels responsible for the solution that is to be implemented."

"Does this come from participation?"

Krishna said, "Absolutely. Participation and involvement in solution development is the key thing. And also, team participation in project decision making. This leads to facilitative leadership in project and program management and other leadership areas and also facilitates self-organizing team emergence."

Arjuna said, "I suppose all this is helped if there is a learning environment?"

"Correct."

"How is this motivation made apparent?"

"When you see individuals and the team going the extra mile to meet commitments."

Krishna continued. "You know, one of the key things is for individuals to be motivated enough to multi-skill themselves to meet project commitments."

Arjuna said, "Well, this is apparent in the football situation. As you said before, a defensive player should be skilled enough to take the ball to the goal and score if the right opportunity presents itself. So, he has to motivate himself to multi-skill himself so that the team overall can benefit. Of course, his career also gets a good boost. But I am not able to see how an individual in a software project context will be motivated to multi-skill himself. What is in it for him?"

Krishna said, "You just explained it. You said that for a football player it helps him get a career boost. This same thing applies in a project context. Self-growth will be the main motivation factor. And, of course, self-interest."

Krishna continued, "Whew, that was an intensive discussion session. What vital sign do you plan to take up next?"

"Should it not be Engineering Excellence?"

"Yes. That is a good choice."

While they were discussing and summarizing these aspects of a Goal-Focused Team, one of the project managers under Arjuna came running to his office.

Bhanumati was going crazy. Her customer had again asked her to change the product. This was the third time this was happening. Each time they got somewhere with the development, the customer would come in with a major change. Each time they had to go back and revisit the design and the development. They were far behind in their schedule.

Bhanumati was the project manager of project Parivartanavyuha. This project was to develop the user interface to the defense system of the city. Each time the customer showed the design to different users, they came back with requests for change.

In desperation, she decided to appeal to Arjuna.

Arjuna asked, "Okay, Bhanumati, what is the problem?"

"My customer is driving me nuts. We have already revamped the design fully twice. Now they want it changed again."

"What do they want changed?"

"Some parts of the user interface."

"But if they only want some parts changed, why can't you just do that?"

"But, the whole user interface needs redesign."

"Oh, I see."

Bhanumati said, "I feel before we complete the design, they are going to ask for another change!"

Krishna told Arjuna, "Arjuna, this is exactly one of the situations where the team can be completely thrown off focus. They are just not able to focus on the goal."

Arjuna turned back to Bhanumati. "I understand your frustration, Bhanumati. Leave this with me. Let me take this up with the customer and get back to you."

Bhanumati went back to her office, relieved that the matter was in Arjuna's capable hands.

Krishna said, "You handled the situation well. You acted like a responsible manager. Management that is completely engaged with the project will insulate teams from such major issues. This needs to be handled at a higher level than the person she is dealing with."

Arjuna said, "My question is, if this is such an evolving product, are they using the right approach? I mean, won't an Agile-based approach be best for such an evolving product?"

"You may have a point. You will need to talk to the customer on this."

Arjuna said, "Yes. I will. I will set up a meeting immediately with my customer counterpart."

Summing up Goal-Focused Team

Arjuna and Krishna summarized the details of Goal Focused Team for Yudhishthira.

Components	Manifestations
Clarity and alignment of individual goals	Relationship between project goals and individual performance goals is discussed and agreed up front Relationship between work targets and project goals is well-understood Individual project performance has a significant bearing on overall performance
Well-equipped team	Provision of project-specific training, mentoring and multi-skilling of team members including the Project Manager and Leads Team-building activities in the project

Components	Manifestations
	Coaching the team to achieve project goals
	Team responds well to a coaching style of management
Team work	Project environment fosters open disagreement
	Conflicts are resolved effectively
	Mutual encouragement within team
	Proactive assistance within team
	Information sharing in the project
	Ownership and a sense of urgency
Learning team	Project experiences are captured and analyzed to identify lessons learned
	Project learns from other projects and shares learning with other projects
	Project exploits re-use
	Project learns from sources external to the organization
	Scope for experimentation
	Application of learning for improved performance (efficiency & effectiveness in achieving project goals)
	Organization fosters a learning culture

Components	Manifestations
Motivated self	Understanding of individual differences in motivation
	Actions are taken to address factors for individual motivation
	Clarity of career path and ownership by individual
	Facilitation of project manager for individual career progression
	The desire to overcome hurdles and obstacles to be successful
	Effective organizational enablers exist for individual career progression
Motivation in the project context	Team involvement in solution development and validation
	Team participation in project decision making
	Learning opportunity in the project for individuals
	Celebrating even small successes
	Individuals multi-skill effectively to meet commitments
	The team goes the extra mile to meet commitments

Chapter 4
Engineering Excellence
Engineering of the Product

The HR department of Pandava Solutions had organized a 10K run for that weekend. Arjuna signed up.

That Saturday morning, they all met outside their office building. The run would take them through three parks and some quiet residential neighborhoods. The run would end where it started.

Arjuna found himself running next to Bhima, the quality assurance director. Bhima was a man who watched his health, and running this 10K race was a simple everyday thing for him. Arjuna was happy that he had such a competent pacemaker.

While Arjuna started panting a bit after the first kilometer, Bhima had not even worked up a sweat. Arjuna plodded on.

After the first kilometer, Bhima turned to Arjuna and asked, "How's Program Kurukshetra going?"

"Pretty well," Arjuna panted.

"What about the work with the vital signs? I heard that you have been trying to put together some kind of a framework to forecast and assure project outcomes. Have you been able to define all the vital signs and their details?"

Arjuna envied Bhima his health. "Not yet fully. I have been able to detail out two vital signs."

"What are they?"

"Customer Connect and Goal-Focused Team."

"Okay. These are the correct ones to start with."

"The next most important vital sign, I think, is Engineering Excellence."

Bhima perked up his ears. "Ah, that is my area. This is clearly one of the key areas of a project. How the product is engineered."

"What do you think are the main features of this?"

"Engineering Excellence comes from how well you are implementing practices and methodologies. An Agile development project will necessarily be different from a non-Agile approach driven project."

"Let us take the non-Agile approach."

Bhima listed the various factors that form and influence the engineering quality of such a non-Agile project.

While panting, Arjuna formed a mental image of what Bhima was saying.

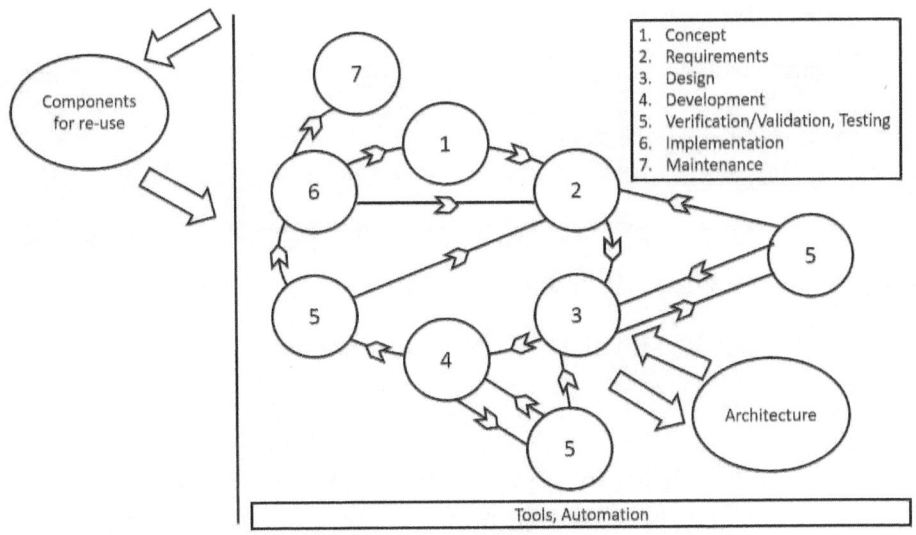

By the time Bhima finished explaining what he was thinking about, they had reached the end of their 10K run. They had taken slightly over one hour and ten minutes. Seven minutes a km was not too bad. Arjuna marveled at Bhima's stamina. He was able to explain the whole area of engineering to Arjuna while running at a decent clip. Arjuna knew that if Bhima had not had Arjuna tagging along, he would have done it faster.

Arjuna decided that he had to tackle this vital sign, Engineering Excellence, and for this he would need to talk to a project team.

Understanding Requirements

The project Arjuna chose was Kurmavyuha. The product from this project allowed for creating the required cyber security for the defense system.

The project manager was Nakula.

Arjuna met him in his office. "Hi, Nakula. How are you?"

"I am okay, Arjuna. And you?"

Arjuna gave Nakula a brief idea about the vital signs and how he was trying to put together a set of components and manifestations for the vital sign "Engineering Excellence."

"I want to use your project to analyze the vital sign Engineering Excellence."

"Sure. My team and I will help you in any way we can."

Arjuna gave Nakula a rundown of what he and Bhima had discussed and drew out the mental image he had formed in his mind.

Nakula said, "I can talk about the requirements."

Arjuna waited.

Nakula said, "One thing that my project and I were fortunate with was that our team has the domain knowledge to understand the requirements."

"Why do you say you are fortunate?"

"In my previous project, this was a big problem. Nobody in the team had the domain knowledge to understand the requirements fully."

Arjuna said, "Okay. This is important. But does the team have the skills and knowledge to elicit and understand the non-functional and any implicit requirements? I find this to be a major problem with many projects."

"Yes, thankfully they do."

"What about priorities among requirements? Are these clear?"

"Yes. The list of requirements, their inter-relationships and priorities are clearly agreed upon and documented."

"Are these requirements clear and visible to all stakeholders?"

"Yes. They are, and we have established a good communication channel with the stakeholders for timely clarification of the requirements."

Arjuna suddenly remembered the conversation he had with Uttara of the Chakravyuha project. He asked Nakula, "What about unstated needs? How are you ensuring that these are indeed taken care of?"

Nakula said, "We are very careful about this. One of the unstated requirements, in the area of cyber security, we feel, is the need to educate citizens about phishing and other threats through on-line training. To ensure that we are implementing these requirements properly, we make frequent releases of usable software in this area so that the implementation can be tested by the user through the building process."

Arjuna was impressed. This project had covered one area of Engineering Excellence really well.

"Thank you, Nakula. I will come back to you if I have any further questions. I will be talking to some of your team leaders and engineers to get further input into this vital sign."

"You are welcome, Arjuna. I will inform my team members."

Nakula was a simple, no-nonsense man. But very competent.

Arjuna met Krishna to apprise him of the discussion he had with Nakula.

"I was talking to Nakula to try to pin down one of the components of Engineering Excellence. He suggested the area of requirements."

"All right, were you able to pin down the components and manifestations?"

"I think so. Nakula was very succinct. I was able to go directly to the manifestations from the conversation."

"What are the manifestations?"

He gave Krishna a summary of the conversation and listed the manifestations.

Component:

Understanding requirements

Manifestations:

- "Adequate domain expertise exists in the team to understand the intended product requirements.

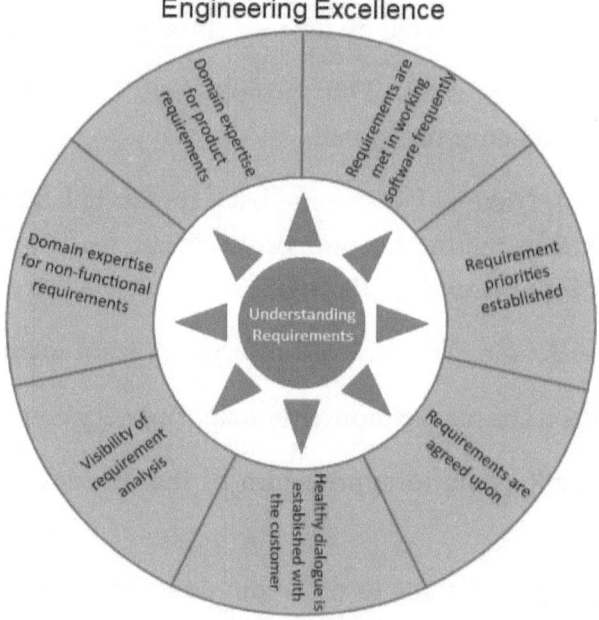

- Adequate domain expertise exists in the team to understand non-functional requirements and elicit requirements that may be implicit.
- There is visibility of requirement analysis & clarifications to stakeholders.

106 | Software Project Health: An Epic Retold

- Healthy dialogue is established with the customer/product owner for timely clarification of requirements.
- List of requirements and their inter-relationships are documented and agreed upon.
- Requirement priorities are clearly established and understood.
- Requirements are met in working software frequently to validate the team's understanding and to unearth unstated needs."

Sound Design, Development and Testing Capability

It was late evening. Arjuna had been working the whole day to put out a fire in one of the projects in the Kurukshetra Program. He had fixed a 7 p.m. meeting with one of the module leaders of the Kurmavyuha project. He knew he would be late for the meeting. When he called the module leader, Sharmishtha, she was sure that she could wait for him. She lived nearby, and getting home late was not a problem for her.

It was 9 p.m. when he sauntered on to the floor where Sharmishtha was waiting for him. She had booked a meeting room for them to meet.

Arjuna did not have to tell her why he was late. She already knew. "All problems with the Gardabhavyuha project sorted out?"

"Yes. Do you know that we almost lost all of the code written so far in the project? Would have been a catastrophe."

"Almost the kind of problem you would not even wish on the Kauravas!"

Arjuna relaxed. He liked her sense of humor.

She asked, "How did they manage to finally salvage the code?"

"Well, keep this to yourself. It would not be nice if the customer came to know of this. One of the engineers had taken a copy of the code on a disk two days ago, when he wanted to make some changes to the code. He had some problem checking his code in. So, he thought there was some problem, and he took his backup. Highly irregular. But it saved the day. Of course, the team needs to redo two days of work."

"Why did the code vanish? Why did the backup not work?"

"We are investigating this."

Sharmishtha looked worried. "I hope our code is safe."

"It is. We have made sure of that." He thought of his conversation with Uttara and Nakula. "You know, Sharmishtha, this is where the need for addressing implied and unstated needs of the customer arises."

"Yes, that is true. This need is required to be addressed regardless of the domain we are working in."

"Yes."

"What is the difference between implied and unstated needs?"

"Well, the need to take backups of your code is an unstated need. No customer is going to tell you that all the code you create for them needs to be backed up regularly. However, in that unstated need is a requirement that you not only take the back up, but you also test the backup to make sure that it works when needed."

"Okay, I get it."

Arjuna then told her of his mission.

"I have already talked to your project leader, Nakula. He gave me a good idea about the requirements handling cycle. I thought that I could talk to you about the design, development and testing cycles."

"Okay. Where shall I start?"

"Tell me about the capabilities of your team in these areas."

"I think my team is fairly capable in the development and testing areas."

"What about design?"

"Ah, we have a small problem there. I think the problem is due to the fact that most of the engineers in my team are not very experienced."

"How do you then overcome this problem?"

Sharmishtha said, "We have trained our design group well. They are now adequate. One saving grace is that the team follows the established design standards and practices carefully."

"Do the design people have domain knowledge to understand the requirements and to do the design properly?"

"Yes. They have good domain knowledge. It is the design skills that can do with some improvement."

"Yeah. Something is better than nothing!?"

"Right."

"Do the testing and development team also follow standards properly?"

"They do."

Arjuna asked, "How good is the project environment?"

"Meaning?"

"The environment for development, validation testing, etc. You know, the workstations, the sandbox, the testing servers, etc."

Sharmishtha said, "They are very good. I would say that we have a good environment. The other thing is that our tools and techniques for development, testing and validation are good, and there is sufficient expertise available to use these effectively."

"Okay. What about expertise in supporting tools like configuration management system, source control systems, test management tools, etc.?"

"These are also adequate."

Arjuna asked, "And does the project team, even if they are inexperienced, show the innovation and patience to adopt new technologies for performance enhancement?"

"Absolutely."

"Thanks, Sharmishtha. You have been a great help."

Arjuna met Krishna to discuss and summarize his discussions with Sharmishtha.

Krishna asked, "What was the main area of discussions with Sharmishtha?"

"We talked about design, development and testing. She felt that while the team was good in development and testing, they had some issues in design."

"Why was that?"

"Mainly because the team was not experienced enough."

"Well, these three areas are important."

Arjuna said, "Okay, so, this can be the component. And the expertise in the area can be the first manifestation."

"Good."

"A lot depends on the team following the standards and practices."

"Yes. Did not the team do that well?"

Arjuna said, "Yes."

"What could be the next manifestation?"

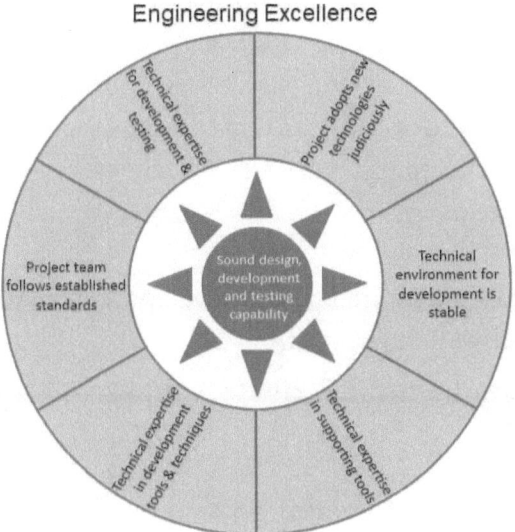

"The next thing is the strength of the environment and the ability to use tools and platforms. And also, re-use. This is happening well with this team."

"Good."

"Well, I think the only other thing is if the team is able to adopt and adapt to new technologies for the good of the project."

"You have got it all down neatly, Arjuna."

"Okay. Shall I summarize?"

"Yes."

Component:

Sound design, development & testing capability

Manifestations:

- "Adequate technical expertise exists in the project development/test environment to meet project goals.

- Project team follows established standards and practices in design, development and testing.
- Adequate technical expertise exists in design, development and testing tools & techniques employed in the project.
- Adequate technical expertise exists in supporting tools (configuration management, source control, test management, etc.).
- Technical environment for development/testing/validation is stable and well-supported.
- Project judiciously adopts new technologies to improve capability to deliver."

Robust Verification and Validation

Arjuna and Krishna were walking along the corridor when they saw a few testers of one of the projects in the Kurukshetra Program hazing one of the managers.

One of them asked the manager, "Heard this joke?"

"What joke?"

"This one:

A group of managers were given the assignment of measuring the height of a flagpole. So, they go out to the flagpole with ladders and tape measures, and they're struggling to get the correct measurement; dropping the tape measures and falling off the ladders.

A tester comes along and sees what they're trying to do, walks over, pulls down the flagpole, lays it flat, measures it from end to end, gives the measurement to one of the managers and walks away.

After the tester is gone, one manager turns to another and laughs, 'Isn't that just like a tester? We're looking for the height and he gives us the length.'

Ha, Ha."

The manager appeared discomfited.

When Krishna and Arjuna came there, the testers paid their respects to them.

Krishna asked the testers, "What is the difference between verification and validation?"

One of them said, "Well, I think they both address the need to ensure that the product that is created is as per specification and what the customer needs?"

Krishna said, "Well, that is the difference! Verification is making sure that the product meets specifications, while validation is ensuring that the product meets customer needs."

The testers appeared a bit confused.

Arjuna said, "In a traditional project, I suppose verification happens throughout the project, while validation happens after the development of a viable piece of software. In an Agile-based project, small and constant verification and validation loops happen together in each iteration."

"That is right. It is between building the product right versus building the right product."

Arjuna asked them, "Which project do you work in?"

"The Kurmavyuha project."

"Oh, Nakula's project."

"Yes, sir."

"Who is the testing team leader?"

One of them came forward, "I am, Arjuna. My name is Krpa."

"Okay. We want to have a talk with you about the verification and validation process of the Kurmavyuha project."

"Okay, shoot."

Arjuna asked, "How good is our verification and validation process?"

"Well, I would call it robust."

Krishna asked, "A good description. Robust. Why would you call it robust?"

Krpa said, "Well, first of all, we know what the customer wants, and we know how it is supposed to be developed."

"Why is this important?"

"Unless we know what is required to be developed, we cannot validate it properly."

Krishna said, "So you are saying that the 'what,' namely the customer's requirements, and the 'how' of it, namely the way to develop, are both well understood for validating and verifying the deliverables?"

"Yes."

"Why else would you call it robust?"

"The other key thing is that we encourage the development team to have prototypes ready so that the customer can see for sure whether he is getting what he wants early on."

Krishna said, "Okay, so you make sure that you know what the customer wants, and to make sure of this, you create prototypes to validate that he is getting what he wants."

"Exactly."

Krishna said, "Excellent. We are on a good wicket here."

Krpa said, "We also create interim outputs, which can be reviewed by the verification and validation team internally. We then also seek customer feedback to make sure we are on the right track."

"The process is getting better and better."

"All engineering documentation and code are reviewed effectively by our team."

"Okay. And?"

"Any external products or components that need to be integrated or tested against are thoroughly tested independently, before integrating with our platform."

"That is important. Otherwise you would not know if the problem is in the external source or in the internal code."

"Exactly."

Arjuna asked, "How good is the test plan and strategy?"

"The test plan addresses both the functional requirements and the non-functional/technical requirements."

"Good. This means that any implicit requirements like performance, usability, availability and security are addressed."

"Yes. That's right."

Krishna asked, "How good is the testing environment?"

Krpa said, "It is very good and supports all our testing needs. We have up-to-date software and hardware configured correctly; right kind of data with appropriate volume and ability to run controlled tests."

Arjuna said, "What else? How does the customer validate the deliverables?"

Krpa said, "We clearly understand the customer's criteria and process for verifying and validating the deliverables."

He continued, "And most important of all, review of engineering documentation and code are carried out in spirit by the right people."

"In spirit? What does that mean?"

Krpa smiled. "Well what I meant was that the people who do the review do a thorough job rather than a perfunctory one. They implement the spirit of the review process rather than just the letter of the process. For example, if code review indicates a mess, people do not balk at re-factoring it right away. So, the 'spirit' is shown in acting on the review comments pronto."

Arjuna said, "Ah, that is good. The 'spirit' is what is important in implementing any process. I think what you told us is a good summary of your verification and validation practice."

Krishna said, "Good. I think that you do, indeed, have a robust process."

Arjuna and Krishna got back to Arjuna's office to discuss and consolidate their findings on the verification and validation.

Krishna said, "So, I think we have the material to list out all the manifestations of this component."

"What should the component be called?"

"Exactly what Krpa described it as: Robust verification and validation."

"Okay. That is clear."

"Then, we need to look at manifestations on the understanding of the requirements first, then on the prototyping and the interim validation."

"Then I suppose we need a couple on the functional and non-functional requirements?"

"Yes. And one on the review process."

"And one on the external components."

"Of course. And we can round it off by the soundness of the testing platform."

"Right."

Krishna said, "Arjuna, can you summarize this?"

"Okay. Here goes.

Component:

Robust verification and validation

Manifestations:

- "Review of engineering documentation and code are carried out in spirit by the right people.
- Interim outputs of deliverables are created and verified internally prior to seeking customer feedback.
- Product components from external sources are validated and accepted.
- Test strategy adequately addresses the functional requirements.
- Test strategy adequately addresses technical/non-functional requirements.
- Prototypes are created to validate requirements and the soundness of the architecture.
- Development and test environments are adequate to support the verification and validation activities effectively.
- Customer's criteria and process for verifying and validating the deliverables are understood."

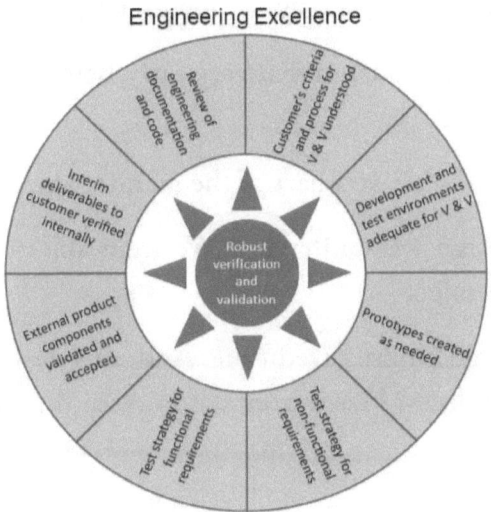

Architecture aspects addressed effectively

Arjuna was alone in his office and thinking. By now, Krishna's coaching had started showing results. Arjuna felt energetic and completely at ease as the manager of the program.

He thought about the vital sign "Engineering Excellence" and its components. He called up Nakula and said, "Nakula, I have a few questions about the background of the project Kurmavyuha."

"Okay, what did you have in mind?"

"How sound is the underlying architecture of the product?"

"It is very good. In fact, it has been reviewed by a panel of experts that included the customer's technology officer and our technology officer."

Arjuna said, "Oh, I see. That is reassuring. What about the team? Does the team have sufficient expertise in the architectural features?"

"Absolutely."

"Does the architecture satisfy the requirements of the customer?"

"Yes. It does. We validated that very early, before we started work on the development."

Arjuna asked, "Were you part of the architecture design?"

"Yes. The design was quite easy. We were able to re-use elements from a previous project."

"Okay. That must have saved time. And, this design can be re-used later for future projects? Has it been designed in that fashion?"

"Yes."

"Thank you, Nakula. You have been very helpful."

When he met Krishna next, he summarized his findings.

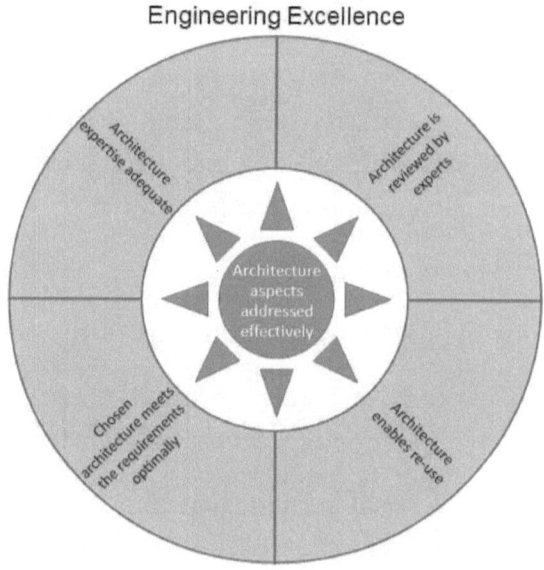

Component:

Architecture aspects addressed effectively

Manifestations:

- Architecture related expertise is adequate in the project.
- Chosen architecture meets the requirements in an optimal way and is validated early in the lifecycle.
- Architecture enables re-use.
- Architecture is reviewed by a panel of experts and architectural risks are identified.

Achieving Technical Quality Requirements

Arjuna was talking to Krtavarman, the team leader of the performance engineering group of Kurmavyuha.

Krishna had asked Arjuna to look at this aspect of Engineering Excellence. Arjuna had talked to Nakula who had directed him to talk to Krtavarman.

"Hello, Krtavarman. How are you?"

"I am well, Arjuna. How can I help you?"

"I am trying to figure out how well we are addressing the technical requirements in this project."

"Okay, this must be part of your looking for vital signs?"

"Yes. And, right now, I am looking at Engineering Excellence."

"Okay. What do you want to know?"

"How are we achieving technical quality requirements?"

Krtavarman asked, "What do you mean by technical quality requirements?"

"You know, there may be a need for high performance – maybe throughput, maybe response time; there may be a need for high levels of security for some pieces of code; some parts of the code may require more rigorous test coverage, etc. You get my drift?"

Krtavarman said, "Yes. I get it – non-functional requirements. This is exactly what our group does. We take code created by others and make sure, where required, these special needs are addressed."

Arjuna asked, "Good. How do you do this?"

"Well, first of all, we have established a benchmark of the technical needs of each component of the product that we are developing."

Arjuna said, "Hold it. Let us talk of the architecture and design. This is the primary requirement. Do the architecture and design adequately address meeting product technical quality requirements?"

Krtavarman said, "Yes. I understand that they do. I inquired on this when I started on this project. It looks like the designers looked at this aspect well."

Arjuna said, "Okay. Good. You were talking about establishing a benchmark…"

Krtavarman said, "Yes. Let us say that 'maintainability' is one of the requirements. In this case, we look at the volume of code (the more voluminous, the more difficult to maintain), redundancy of code (duplicated code needs change in more than one place), coupling (tight coupling of components make them difficult to maintain), complexity (the more complex, the more difficult to maintain) and unit sizes of the code (the smaller, the better)."

"Good, I understand."

"So, you establish these benchmarks. Then what?"

"Then we establish baselines for each of these. Also, any code being re-used is subject to these benchmarks before changing it."

"Okay. Next?"

"Then we work with the development team to ensure that the developed code meets these technical requirements. Or, if they do not, we send the code back to the development team to make the necessary corrections."

"Okay. This makes sense."

Krtavarman said, "The next step is to ensure that the code's technical quality is measured as early as possible so that expensive rewrite becomes unnecessary."

Arjuna said, "Good. So, you have the right process to ensure technical quality."

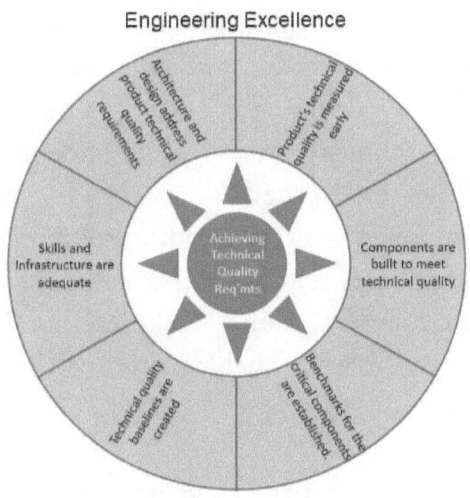

Krtavarman said, "Of course, before all this, we have to ensure that our engineers in development, through training and experience, have the necessary skills to understand all this to implement it. Also, we have to ensure the right infrastructure and automation. You know, tools, platforms, etc."

"Excellent. This is great. You seem to have got this under control."

"Thanks. Please come back to me if you need anything else."

When Arjuna met Krishna next, he updated him on his discussions with Krtavarman. Krishna was happy with the outcome. He asked Arjuna to summarize his discussions.

Component:

Achieving Technical Quality Requirements

Manifestations:

- Architecture and design adequately address meeting product technical quality requirements.
- Skills and infrastructure (tools, processes, techniques…) are adequate to measure product technical quality.
- Technical quality baselines are created for existing code prior to enhancements, and extent of improving the existing code is determined.
- Benchmark technical quality requirements for the critical components are established.
- Critical components of the product/solution are built to meet the technical quality requirements.
- Overall product's/solution's technical quality is measured as early as possible to enable meeting the technical quality requirements.

Engineering Practices - Re-use, Tools and Automation

That morning when Arjuna walked into his office, Yudhishthira's admin was waiting for him. He informed Arjuna that Yudhishthira wanted to meet him urgently. Arjuna obeyed the summons.

When he reached Yudhishthira's office, he found that Yudhishthira had company. Yudhishthira introduced them to each other. The person, Karna, in Yudhishthira's office was the works manager of the largest automobile plant in the country.

Yudhishthira said, "Do you know why I called you here? Karna here can give you some insights into the need for automation in any process."

Karna said, "Yes. Automation is the key to the success of any process. And you know that any factory or plant thrives on automation."

Yudhishthira said, "Yes, gaining efficiencies through automation is the key to a successful plant."

Arjuna asked, "Sir, what are the benefits of automation?"

Karna said, "Some of the benefits are: Reduced production cost, decreased cycle time, improved quality and reliability, well-utilized floor space, reduced waste, and thus, the ability to stay competitive."

Karna continued, "Some of the disadvantages are loss of versatility, higher levels (sometimes) of pollution, large initial investment, increase in unemployment and sometimes unforeseen costs."

Yudhishthira said, "Software development too can benefit from automation. Especially the area of testing and also deployment."

Arjuna said, "Yes. I can see that. Some of the advantages of automated testing are speed, repeatability, reusability, reliability and comprehensiveness. And some of the advantages of automated deployment are deployments become much less error-prone and much more repeatable; anyone can deploy software; engineers can focus on development; painless deployment to new sites and more frequent release."

Karna was impressed. "Yes. You are right, absolutely."

Yudhishthira said, "I want you to start thinking of automation as one of the key components of the Engineering Excellence vital sign. This is why I called you here."

When Arjuna said goodbye and left them, he was in a thinking mood. Yes. Automation was a key component of Engineering Excellence. He knew he had to talk to Krishna.

Krishna agreed with Arjuna that automation was one of the key components of Engineering Excellence.

He said, "I think you should consider the whole area of engineering practices: Reuse, use of tools and automation together."

Arjuna said, "Okay. How do we do this?"

"Let us go to Nakula and talk to him about how he achieves this."

Nakula was happy to see them. He knew that Arjuna was making good progress in the Engineering Excellence vital sign using inputs from his project.

Krishna asked, "Nakula, we want to talk about your engineering practices. You know, reuse, use of tools, automation, etc."

"Good. What do you want to know?"

"Tell us about reuse. How well do you reuse components?"

Nakula said, "Before we started the project, we looked at the reuse library to see what was available. We make it a practice before we start coding each piece of software, to see if anything already available can be reused."

"How do you decide if something can be reused?"

"We look for modular, uncoupled code that addresses one function or one unit and is possibly standalone with clean APIs. If the code is too complicated, we try to avoid it, since there may be too much work needed on it. We also make sure that we use only fully tested code, which does what it is supposed to be doing. We also run extensive tests on it before we accept it."

"What percentage of your current project code is based on reused code?"

"I think about 25%."

"This is good."

Nakula continued, "We also make a conscious effort to ensure whatever code we write is reusable by other projects."

Arjuna said, "Excellent. Tell me about your usage of tools."

"We use tools for quality verification."

"What kind of tools?"

"Mainly static analysis testing tools. These tools analyze code for bugs, for weaknesses, for security flaws, unused code, redundant code, for maintainability, etc. We have tools that work on uncompiled source code and also on the object code."

"What about unit testing tools?"

"Here again, we use many tools. These tools provide for planning and designing test cases, test data provisioning, coverage, etc."

Engineering Excellence | 127

Krishna said, "What about system and integration testing tools?"

Nakula said, "Our testing process is fully automated. We have a fully automated test environment that includes applications, test data, database server, front-end and back-end environments, hardware, network and documentation required."

"Very comprehensive."

"Yes. It is very comprehensive. This environment allows for smoke tests, regression tests and other kinds of tests."

Krishna was very impressed. "This project is doing well in the engineering practices department. I have only two more things in mind. Build setup and configuration management."

Nakula said, "We use very robust build and configuration management tools. Our tools take care of every step of the delivery process – from the provisioning of physical and virtual machines, to reporting code development through testing, updates and product release. They ensure stability, reliability and consistency. They also aid close collaboration between developers and sys-admins, enabling more efficient delivery of code."

Krishna looked at Arjuna, "I think you have a good project here. Their engineering practices are excellent. You will not have any problem with this project on this front."

Krishna and Arjuna got back to Krishna's office.

Krishna said, "It was a good meeting with Nakula. I learned a lot of things."

"Yes, Nakula describes things very concisely and without exaggeration."

"Right. So, the component of vital sign Engineering Excellence is 'Engineering Practices – Re-use, Tools & Automation.'"

Arjuna said, "Okay. Let me summarize this."

Component:

Engineering Practices – Re-use, Tools & Automation

Manifestations:

- Re-using from other projects.
- Contributing to re-use.
- Code quality verification is achieved by fully exploiting tools.
- Unit testing effectiveness & coverage are achieved through best use of tools.
- Smoke test scenarios are scripted for automation and are executed when required.
- Regression test scenarios are scripted for automation and are executed when required.
- Build management practices and tooling are effective in supporting integrity of the components and agility requirements of release commitments.
- Configuration management practices and tooling are effective in supporting integrity of the components and enabling effective build management.
- Test environment set-up is automated.
- Test data population is automated.

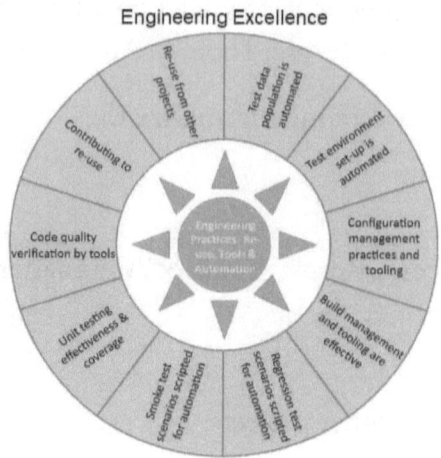

Krishna said, "Good. This is well put."

Summarizing Engineering Excellence

Arjuna and Krishna summarized the details of the vital sign Engineering Excellence for Yudhishthira.

Components	Manifestations
Understanding requirements	Adequate domain expertise exists in the team to understand the intended product requirements
	Adequate domain expertise exists in the team to understand non-functional requirements and elicit requirements that may be implicit
	Visibility of requirement analysis & clarifications to stakeholders
	Healthy dialogue is established with the customer/product owner for timely clarification of requirements
	List of requirements and their inter-relationships are documented and agreed upon

Components	Manifestations
	Requirement priorities are clearly established and understood
	Requirements are met in working software frequently to validate the team's understanding and unearthing unstated needs
Sound design, development & testing capability	Adequate technical expertise exists in the project development/test environment to meet project goals
	Team follows established standards and practices in design, development and testing
	Adequate technical expertise exists in design, development and testing tools & techniques employed in the project
	Adequate technical expertise exists in supporting tools (configuration management, source control, test management, etc.)
	Technical environment for development/testing/validation is stable and well-supported
	Project judiciously adopts new technologies to improve capability to deliver
Robust verification and validation	Review of engineering documentation and code are carried out in spirit by the right people
	Interim outputs of deliverables are created and verified internally prior to seeking customer feedback
	Product components from external sources are validated and accepted

Components	Manifestations
	Test strategy adequately addresses the functional requirements
	Test strategy adequately addresses technical/non-functional requirements
	Prototypes are created to validate requirements and the soundness of the architecture
	Development and test environments are adequate to support the verification and validation activities effectively
	Customer's criteria and process for verifying and validating the deliverables is understood
Architecture aspects addressed effectively	Architecture-related expertise is adequate in the project
	Chosen architecture meets the requirements in an optimal way and is validated early in the lifecycle
	Architecture enables re-use
	Architecture is reviewed by a panel of experts and architectural risks are identified
Achieving Technical Quality Requirements	Architecture and design address product technical quality requirements
	Skills and infrastructure (tools, processes and techniques) are adequate to measure product technical quality
	Technical quality baselines are created for existing code prior to enhancements and the extent of improving existing code is determined

Components	Manifestations
	Benchmark technical quality requirements for the critical components are established
	Critical components of the product/solution are built to meet the technical quality requirements
	Overall product's/solution's technical quality is measured as early as possible to enable meeting the technical quality requirements
Engineering Practices – Re-use, Tools & Automation	Re-using from other projects
	Contributing to re-use
	Code quality verification is achieved by fully exploiting tools
	Unit testing effectiveness & coverage are achieved through use of tools
	Smoke test scenarios are scripted for automation and are executed when required
	Regression test scenarios are scripted for automation and are executed when required
	Build management practices and tooling are effective in supporting integrity of components and agility requirements of releases
	Configuration management practices and tooling are effective in supporting integrity of the components and enabling effective build management
	Test environment set-up is automated
	Test data population is automated

Chapter 5

Execution Excellence

Without Execution, "Vision" Is Just Another Word for Hallucination

Arjuna had been invited for a drink with Draupadi. It was not often that Draupadi invited program managers for this honor. She had been hearing good things about the Kurukshetra Program, and she had been impressed with Arjuna during their first meeting.

Draupadi had chosen a fancy bar near their office for their meeting. Normally, Arjuna would not have gone to this bar. It was too expensive. But, Draupadi preferred this one since they could talk without being disturbed by loud music and a rambunctious crowd.

"How are you, Arjuna? I have been hearing good things about you."

"I am OK, thanks."

Draupadi ordered a gin and tonic, and Arjuna ordered a beer.

"How is the Kurukshetra Program going?"

"It is going well. As I had told you before, when we met last time, I have been trying to figure out a good way to assess the health of the constituent projects. I want to ensure that I will be able to tell if they are really going all right."

"What areas have you covered so far?"

"I have looked at the following areas or vital signs as we call them…"

"Yes, I know about the vital signs that you are looking at."

"Yes, I have looked at measuring the following vital signs – Customer Connect, Goal-Focused Team and Engineering Excellence."

"These are good areas to start with. Have you heard of a person called Mark Hurd?"

"Yes, is he not the CEO of Oracle?"

"Yes. He is the co-CEO of Oracle. He had once made a remark, 'Without execution, "vision" is just another word for hallucination.'"

"That's interesting. Are you suggesting that I take up the area of Execution Excellence next?"

"Yes. Excellence in execution is one of the key vital signs you should measure to check whether a project is healthy."

"Madam, now that I think about it, you are right. I was thinking that once all the other aspects like Customer Connect, a focused team and Engineering Excellence are in place, excellence in execution would automatically be obtained."

"Yes, it is easy to fall into that trap. I have discovered during the many years I have led programs that if you take your eyes off the execution ball, you are likely to lose your project wicket. I remember one project where… Anyway, let me not bore you with my reminiscences."

Arjuna felt humbled. Even people like Draupadi had a stage in their careers where they were leading projects and programs.

Draupadi continued, "Let me clue you in on one of the areas of Execution Excellence you have to take care of first. I am sure Krishna and the others will help you with this and other areas. One key requirement of Execution Excellence is to have clarity of project goals and success criteria, both short-term and long-term. Without this clarity, whatever is produced will not meet the customer's expectations."

Arjuna asked, "But, won't this be covered during the planning process?"

"It will, to a large extent. However, unless the project team understands the customer's intent, the intricacies of development and implementation will miss the true import of the customer needs."

"I suppose what you are saying is that an engineer who develops code after understanding the customer's long-term and short-term goals will be able to deliver a better customer experience?"

"Exactly. Taking an extreme example, coding for mission critical projects that your program encompasses needs to be different from writing code for an information portal. One unnecessary program traversal through a loop or an extra function call could make a difference in a mission critical system. Understanding the difference and providing for it is one of the hallmarks of Execution Excellence."

"Okay. I think I am starting to understand why it is important that one key area of Execution Excellence is understanding project goals and success criteria."

Draupadi said, "First talk to the project manager and team and understand what their thinking is. This can help you formulate the components of the vital sign."

"Thank you, Ma'am."

Clarity of Project Goals and Success Criteria - Short-term and Long-term

One of the key constituent projects of Program Kurukshetra was Samyojana. It was a large project with over fifty highly skilled engineers on it. The project involved developing and implementing the platform to integrate the working of all the constituents of the defensive net around Hastinapura. Once this platform is implemented and integrated, it would be impossible for anyone to penetrate the city's defenses.

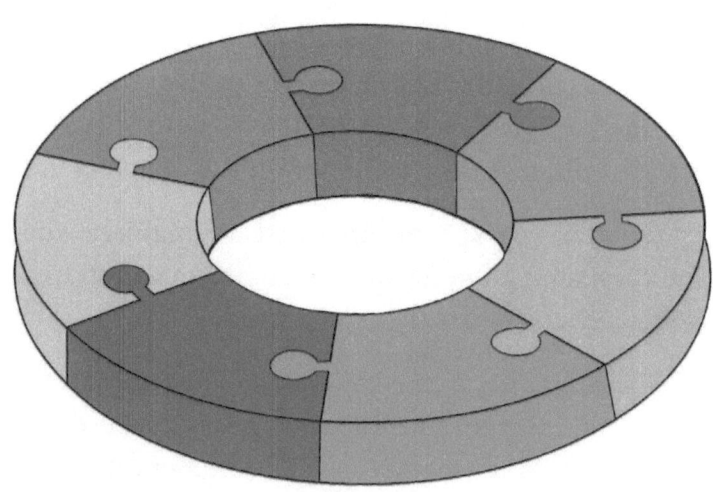

The project manager in charge of this project was Sahadevi. She was not as experienced as the other project managers, but she was selected by Yudhishthira since she came to Pandava Solutions highly recommended by one of his colleagues. And, she was proving to be worth the faith reposed in her.

She was an easy-going, friendly person, and she was on good terms with her team members and the other project managers.

"Sahadevi, how are you?"

"I am great. How's your program management job going? And, have you been able to nail down the vital signs of a project?"

"Not yet. Am still working on that along with my other duties. In fact, right now I am trying to put together the components of the vital sign called Execution Excellence."

"Good. This is one of Draupadi's key interest areas."

Arjuna was surprised. "How do you know this?"

"I sometimes meet and talk to Draupadi in the Pandava Women's Club. She occasionally drops in to cheer us on."

Arjuna was a bit envious. But, he continued, "Sahadevi, I want to talk to one of the team leaders of your project to discuss project success criteria. Who would you recommend that I talk to?"

Sahadevi said, "The leader of the testing team. Her name is Damayanti. She is very smart and is able to articulate her ideas well."

"Okay. Let me talk to her." Arjuna went in search of Damayanti.

"Hi, Damayanti, how are you?"

"Hello, Arjuna. What brings you here?"

"I am trying to put together a framework for assessing the health of projects. I am trying to define a set of parameters whose pulse beats can be sensed to give us an idea of the overall health of a project."

"I see."

"One key vital sign, identified for us by none other than Draupadi, herself, is Execution Excellence."

"Execution excellence?"

"Yes. The execution of a project is measured against the application of the knowledge of the team of the goals of the project."

"Okay. I think I am starting to understand."

Arjuna asked, "Damayanti, do you have a clear idea of the success criteria of the project that you are doing?"

"Yes, I think."

"What are these?"

"Well, meeting the customer's requirements, both explicit and implied, is one key thing. Quality software is another. And great customer experience is another."

"Good. Of course, there may be others. But, these are the most critical. Are you keeping these in mind when your team is developing the product?"

Damayanti said, "Yes. We are."

Arjuna asked, "Damayanti, how do you know that you have clarity of project goals?"

She said, "For one, the project goals and business justification and goals, both short-term and long-term, are properly documented, and our team has access to these documents."

"Okay, good."

Damayanti continued, "Sahadevi is a good project manager. One of the first things we did when we formed the team was to get some of these documents made available to the entire team. We also had a couple of calls and discussions with our customer counterpart to confirm that understanding of project goals and success criteria is the same as what is documented."

"That's interesting."

Damayanti said, "And this has ensured that the entire team, all fifty of us, have a clear idea of the project goals and success criteria."

"Implicit and explicit?"

"Yes. Our customer was quite explicit about an implicit success criterion for us! He wanted to make sure we meet his success criteria which will ensure that he got his bonus for the year!"

Arjuna laughed. "You should have told him to put this in the requirements!"

"Ha!"

"Okay, this is important. We cannot belittle this."

"That is right. And because the customer knows that we understand the goals well, when they review our project, they concentrate on the big things and not the relatively unimportant."

Arjuna said, "I know. In one of the other projects in the program, the customer made a big fuss that the code is not properly indented!"

He continued, "So we know that the project's purpose and business case are well documented and understood by the team."

"Yes."

Arjuna said, "In this case, the business case is life or death for the city, eh?"

Damayanti smiled. "Yes."

Arjuna asked, "Okay. Are the customer's final and intermediate milestones well understood by the team?"

He added flippantly, "Any intermediate bonuses?!"

Damayanti liked the joke. "Yes. We clearly understand the milestones, both final and intermediate."

"How are you sure of that?"

Damayanti said, "As I said before, we have had many discussions with the customer. And we have arrived at a common understanding about this."

Arjuna was getting more and more impressed with Sahadevi and Damayanti. This was exactly what a project should be doing.

He asked, "What if the goals or milestones are not met? Does the team know the impact on the product and the stakeholders? Other than the bonus that is!"

Damayanti smiled, "Yes. We all clearly understand this. If all the defense system constituents are ready but the integration platform is not, it will be very unpleasant when the enemy attacks."

"Yes. And the Kauravas will walk away with the prize."

"If they are alive!"

"That's right. We know the impact of not meeting our milestones."

Arjuna said, "Thanks, Damayanti. I think I am clear on why this project is going well. I also understand the manifestations when there is clarity of the project goals and success criteria."

Damayanti said, "Arjuna, there is another important thing that you seem to have missed out."

Arjuna was surprised. "What is it?"

"You know, the customer and Sahadevi have a process by which the team and team members are recognized when they meet the milestones successfully. This is very important."

"Of course! You are right. Without this incentive, the enthusiasm of the team will be dampened. This incentive was approved due to the criticality of the integration platform."

"Right. You may want to consider similar schemes for other projects as well."

"Thanks, you have been a great help. Keep up the good work on the project."

"Okay. Bye."

When Arjuna met Krishna next, he was in an elated mood. His encounter with Damayanti and project Samyojana had left him in a positive frame of mind.

Krishna asked, "You look happy. What gives?"

Arjuna said, "Well, I had a very interesting meeting with Damayanti, one of the team leaders of project Samyojana led by Sahadevi."

"Okay. And?"

"The story starts before that. I had meeting, over a drink, with Draupadi."

"Draupadi invited you for a drink? That's great. She does not extend that honor to many people. You have arrived. What happened at the meeting?"

"The gist of it was that she advised me to take up the area of Execution Excellence next."

"That's good. I was also thinking along those lines."

"After that, I met up with Damayanti. We discussed the area of success criteria and project goals. She had a clear understanding of what these are and could articulate them well. I have a warm fuzzy feeling about this project and the team."

Krishna asked, "So you are saying that Clarity of project goals and success criteria – short-term and long-term – is one of the key components of the vital sign Execution Excellence?"

"Yes."

He then gave Krishna a very brief summary of his discussions with Damayanti. Krishna was happy. He felt that the discussions had thrown up the right manifestations for the component.

He said, "Can you list the manifestations for the component?"

"Yes."

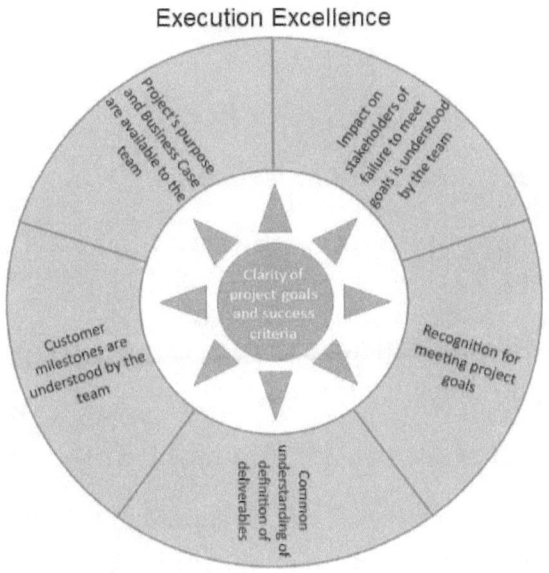

Project's purpose and business case are well documented and available for the team

Customer milestones (short term and long term) are well-understood

There is common understanding between the customer and the team on the definition of deliverables for each milestone

There is recognition for meeting the goals successfully

Impact to stakeholders of failure to meet goals is well understood by the team

Krishna said, "You have summed this up quite well."

"Thank you, Krishna."

Krishna said, "The next area you should look at is how well the estimates have been done for the project. Were the estimates done taking into account the ability of the team to deliver?"

"Okay. Let us take this area up next."

"Samyojana seems to be an interesting project. I will come along when you meet them next."

"Okay."

Estimates Reflect Capability to Deliver

Arjuna had arranged to have a meeting with Sahadevi the next day to further discuss the Execution Excellence vital sign.

Accordingly, they met in Sahadevi's office the next morning. Krishna also accompanied Arjuna for the meeting.

Sahadevi welcomed them, "Hi, Arjuna; hi, Krishna. Welcome."

Arjuna said, "Hi, Sahadevi. I had a very enlightening discussion with Damayanti yesterday. She feels that you are a good project manager."

Sahadevi felt uncomfortable. Some people cannot take praise easily. She was one such.

"Well, I try to do the best that I can. And, Damayanti is good. In fact, I think she is better than me."

Arjuna let that go.

Krishna said, "Your project is seen as one of the most important parts of the Kurukshetra Program. It is good to know that it is going well."

Arjuna said, "Sahadevi, you are aware of how we are trying to put together a framework for project health assessment."

"Yes. I am aware. I know that you are looking at exploring the vital sign Execution Excellence with the Samyojana Project."

"That is right. And one of the components of this vital sign that Krishna recommends that we take up next is the area of estimation."

"Okay, how do you want to start?"

Krishna said, "The question is this: Is the ability of the project team to deliver commensurate with the estimates? That is, did the estimates reflect the capacity of the team to deliver?"

Sahadevi said, "Okay, let me give you my perspective on estimates as far as my project, Samyojana, is concerned. My simple answer to your question is no, estimates for this project do not reflect the capacity to deliver."

Arjuna asked, "Is this because the estimates were wrong or because the team faces some challenges that prevent it from meeting the estimates?"

"I think the estimates were wrong."

"Where did the estimate go wrong, in your opinion?"

"Well, first of all, the estimates did not take into consideration some of the non-functional requirements."

"What do you mean by non-functional requirements?"

"Things that affect the operation of a system rather than just the functionality. For example, things like response time, stability, etc."

"Which of the non-functional requirements were not adequately provided for?"

"In this case, the non-functional requirement that is not adequately provided for is the time taken to detect that a service is down and initiate a new instance."

Arjuna asked, "Why was this not taken care of?"

"Frankly, I feel that it was not done by people who had the expertise. They have also not documented the estimation assumptions."

Arjuna asked, "How are you overcoming this problem?"

"Well, when I took over this project, I knew that there was a problem, and I informed the then program manager, your predecessor, about it. He was of the opinion that we need to somehow ride over this problem. But I was able to get some specialist engineers assigned to the project. This has helped. And since you, Arjuna, came on to the scene, things have become better. I have been able to get more appropriate resources assigned to the project."

Krishna said, "It is good that you have done this. Arjuna, note that you need to check the other projects also to see if the estimates have been realistic. Other project managers may not have cottoned on to the problems in estimation. They may go along merrily till they suddenly discover that they have a problem."

Arjuna said, "Yes. I have already started doing that. When Sahadevi indicated to me that she had a problem, I took it up with the other projects also."

Krishna said, "Sahadevi, what other problems do you see with estimation?"

"I see two more problems. One is that the estimates did not make any assumption about the tools that we are using."

"Are you saying that there was an overestimation?"

"Yes. Some of the tools we use help us improve our productivity beyond what was assumed during estimation. This has, to some extent, offset the underestimation made when non-functional requirements were not considered. But, not to the extent required, of course."

Krishna said, "Of course, two wrongs do not make a right!"

"Right!"

Sahadevi continued, "And the fact that we have to integrate with a platform that is complicated had not been taken into consideration."

Arjuna said, "When I checked with the Program Management Office, I found that past data from projects and programs have not been used as a basis for estimates. This reinventing of the wheel and reluctance to take past experience into consideration is a problem that needs to be overcome."

Krishna said, "Unless, of course, the available past data or experience was not really applicable to this case?"

"Naturally."

Krishna asked, "Sahadevi. Other than Arjuna, have you taken this estimation issue up with other stakeholders?"

"Yes. I have indicated to the customer the issues we are facing so that there is some appreciation from them about our struggle to meet schedules. I have also brought it up in the Program Steering Committee meeting. The unfortunate thing was that this was not done when the estimates were done. The estimates were not discussed with all the stakeholders and agreed upon."

Krishna said, "This is a problem I have seen in projects across organizations. It is good that Sahadevi has taken it up in the proper forums."

He continued, "Thanks, Sahadevi. I think we understand the situation well now. Let Arjuna know what difficulties you are facing, and I am sure he will work it out with you."

"Thanks, Krishna."

"Bye, Sahadevi."

"Bye, Krishna and Arjuna."

Krishna and Arjuna walked back to Arjuna's office. Krishna said, "Sahadevi seems to be very competent. She is able to put facts on the table without being bitter about it or pointing fingers. Her attitude seems to be 'correct any issues and move forward.'"

"Yes. She is very competent. I seek her inputs and rely on her advice with regards to other projects also."

Krishna said, "Okay. Are we now in a position to discuss and fix the next component of the Execution Excellence vital sign?"

"Yes. I think the component is 'Estimates reflect capability to deliver.'"

"Good. And what are its manifestations?"

Arjuna said, "If we think about what Sahadevi said first, the first manifestation should be 'Inputs to estimation include functional & non-functional requirements, and it is done by people with the required expertise.'"

"Agreed. And as an adjunct manifestation we can say, 'Size is estimated based on the product scope and the nature of work.'"

"Okay. And the estimates should be realistic."

Krishna asked, "Good. What other manifestation can you think of?"

Arjuna said, "One of the items that Sahadevi called to our attention is the fact that the estimates had not taken into consideration integration into a difficult platform."

"Yes, that is right. And the estimates need to keep in mind the capability of the people."

"Okay, so we need to say, 'Effort, cost and duration are derived from size with appropriate considerations for product attributes, platform attributes, tools used and people capability.'"

"That is good. Anything else?"

Arjuna thought, "Well…"

Krishna said, "I refer to the point you brought up. Getting inputs from past data."

"Right. Of course. Past data from the project and the organization are used appropriately to derive predictable estimates."

"That is well put. Sahadevi brought up a point on how she is getting over the problems."

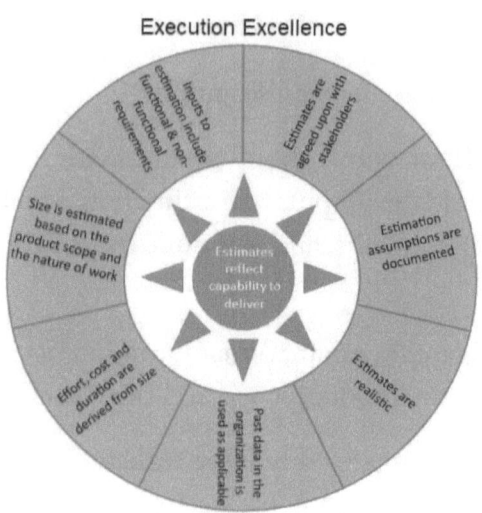

"You mean tracking the assumptions and acting as needed?"

Krishna said, "I think we can say, Estimation assumptions are documented and tracked throughout the project for appropriate actions if they turn out to be false."

"Then there is the issue of discussing the estimates with all stakeholders."

Arjuna said, "Yes. I think we can say: Estimates are agreed upon among stakeholders as appropriate and are used to validate ability to deliver on the commitments. Makes sense?"

"Yes. I think we have this component now nailed down. I think we have covered all the manifestations."

Adaptive Integrated Plans

Sahadevi and her husband were avid golfers. So were Arjuna and his wife. So that Saturday, Arjuna invited Sahadevi and her husband for a day of golf and fun at their golf club. Krishna was also invited.

They had breakfast at the club, and around eleven o' clock, they found that there was no one waiting at the first tee. The five of them grabbed the opportunity.

They were not good golfers, none of the five. But they could get by. Their round took approximately four hours, and they were back by around three for lunch. Sahadevi's husband was by far the best among them, and he beat them all by many strokes. He came twenty above par and the others – well, it is best not said.

During the game, Arjuna and Krishna had a chance to talk to Sahadevi about the planning process of the project.

Arjuna teed off and asked, "Sahadevi, we want to talk to you about your project plans."

Sahadevi said, "All right. Let's. Oh, good shot."

Arjuna asked, "Sahadevi, are you not the person who is responsible for the planning process of the project?"

"Yes."

"How would you describe your project's plan in one phrase?"

"It is adaptive and integrated."

Krishna said, "That is very broad. What do you mean by this?"

"Well it covers all the aspects of the project, and it is so built that it can be adapted in response to any changing need."

Krishna asked with specious guile, "But, Sahadevi, yours is a fixed-price project based on a certain scope covering ALL the requirements, is it not? So, how can you then keep adapting to changing needs and still meet the project's cost goals?"

Sahadevi did not catch on. She smiled and said, "Krishna, it is not an uncommon problem in fixed-price software projects. Am I right, Arjuna?"

Arjuna's rueful smile in response said it all! He asked, "What is your 'adaptiveness' of plans based on?"

Sahadevi said, "Well, first of all, while estimating and bidding, we put in various amounts of effort buffer depending on the assessment of uncertainty."

"Okay. That makes sense. What about any assumptions you make based on your assessment of uncertainty?"

"We document key assumptions about scope which, in many cases, are validated with the customer while agreeing on the fixed price."

Krishna asked, "All right. This, I suppose, will make it easy when you go to the customer with requests for additions to scope and time?"

Sahadevi said, "Correct." She turned to Arjuna. "Arjuna, I gather from Abhimanyu that you have been discussing 'Customer Connect' with his team. Our Customer Connect is in pretty good shape, I believe. The customer understands that there are some pretty complex areas in project Samyojana, and he is quite amenable in those areas to acknowledge increased complexity and provide relief to us in terms of cost and time."

Arjuna said, "This is good. I am happy that project teams are talking to each other and discussing aspects that are important across projects."

Krishna asked, "What if enlargement of work is due to internal reasons and not due to increased scope?"

"Of course, when the scope remains largely the same and only our work expands for various internal reasons, we cannot go back to the customer."

"What do you do then?"

"We can only try and use some automation to reduce work to an extent and, of course, seek management help with more resources."

"And management has been supportive?"

Sahadevi said, "As I told you earlier, management has been quite supportive and have always provided us with specialist help in some areas like non-functional requirements even taking quite a hit on project margins; across the Kurukshetra Program and especially in Samyojana Project, I believe management is very well-engaged to assure success."

Arjuna nodded approvingly and said, "That is good. What else?"

"Our plan has adequate resilience, through multi-skilling, gradual ramp-up, optimal concurrency of tasks, etc., to meet the project goals within the accepted tolerance levels."

"What do you mean by resilience?"

"Ability to bounce back from most adversities to prevent problems from building on each other."

Arjuna asked, "How do you ensure that you notice any indicators of adverse conditions?"

Sahadevi said, "We have identified trigger conditions under which we have to re-plan. For example, a significant change in requirements needed by the customer, missed internal milestone by a sizable period, large slippage in the joining date of a team member, etc."

"What do you have to do then?"

"We then have to interpret these indicators and act on them to recover from these conditions. We also have to put in place actions to contain the effect of these events."

She continued, "We also promptly update the project plan in the event of any risk materializing or an unforeseen event materializing and gain the relevant stakeholder's approval."

Krishna asked, "Okay. How granular are your plans?"

"The plans are just granular enough to meet short-term customer milestones."

Krishna asked, "But, how could you plan at such a detailed level in the beginning. Would enough information have been available?"

By then they had reached the ninth hole. Sahadevi made a good shot.

Sahadevi said, "Good question. No. Details are added as we go along. We practice progressive elaboration to manage the project at detailed levels as we go along. This means we continuously improve our plans as more detailed and specific information and more accurate estimates become available. These improved plans are then discussed with the stakeholders. Of course, we always have the original scope and assumptions in mind while we elaborate and watch out for scope creep, increased work, etc. and work with customers and internal management as I described above."

"Okay, that is a good approach. What about dependencies? Have all the dependencies been identified?"

"Our project plan identifies all external dependencies (upstream) and recognizes others who are externally dependent (downstream) on our planned deliverables. These dependencies are continuously updated and published to the relevant stakeholders."

Krishna asked, "When changes are made to plans, are they reviewed?"

"Yes, sure. Plans are independently reviewed both initially and also when significant changes occur. We do this very diligently."

She continued, "In addition to these reviews when changes happen, we have worked in a set of review points for progress assessment. There is also adequate provision for review of deliverables."

Krishna said, "Okay. One of the problems that project managers commonly face is that technology changes rapidly. They may have worked with a very advanced technology in the last project, but come the current one, better technology has come up. In fact, technology can even change during the course of the project!"

Sahadevi was not beaten. She said, "We take care of that. Our plans are adapted to incorporate new technologies and approaches from the beginning and as the project progresses."

Arjuna asked, "How do the engineers cope with the need for understanding and implementing new technologies and approaches?"

"We do the required multi-skilling for this"

They had reached the last hole. It was clear that Krishna was the winner among them, not considering Sahadevi's husband.

"Congratulations, Krishna. Well done."

"Thanks. Sahadevi, how do you keep track of the plans and the changes?"

"Our planning and tracking are well-supported through the use of the right tools."

"All right. I think we have a good idea of your planning process."

They repaired to the lunch tables for a well-deserved lunch.

That Monday morning, Krishna met Arjuna to summarize the discussions they had with Sahadevi.

Krishna said, "Well, the component that we have now can be called 'Adaptive, integrated plans.'"

"Yes. That is a good way of putting it."

"We can distill out the manifestations of it from the points made by Sahadevi in our discussions."

"Okay."

"First of all, 'Plans exist to address requirements and project goals.'"

Arjuna said, "Okay. I think Sahadevi was clear on that. I think the next should be 'Plans have resilience to meet project goals within tolerance levels.'"

Krishna said, "All right. What's next?"

"Internal milestones are well-defined and granular to meet short-term customer milestones."

"OK. Agreed. Next?"

"Progressive elaboration of the activities is practiced and is accepted by stakeholders."

"Yes. This is very important. Sahadevi was very proud of that. And the next?"

Arjuna said, "Project plans identify dependencies (upstream & downstream) and are shared with appropriate stakeholders."

"All right, I think there are seven more. Can you list them?"

"OK. Here goes. Project plans include review points for progress assessment. Project plan provides for review of deliverables. Trigger conditions are identified which require re-planning. Plans are revised when risks materialize or when unforeseen events occur. Planning and tracking are well-supported through the right tools. Plans are independently reviewed initially and when significant changes occur."

He continued. "And finally, plans are adapted to incorporate new technologies and approaches and the required multi-skilling."

"Good, I think we have nailed down this component of Execution Excellence well."

Timely Equipping of Talent and Provision of Tools & Environment

Madri was the administration officer of the Kurukshetra Program. She and her small team of three were responsible for all the admin, HR and other support work for the program. Her team also liaised with the system resources group to provide all the technical resources needed for the project. She reported to Arjuna.

She and her team were known to be very efficient at what they were doing. Many a time they were trammeled by the lack of resources, but they made do with what was available, and they supported the program admirably.

Arjuna went to meet her next. He wanted to discuss resourcing with her. Arjuna was aware that timely resourcing of the right talent and tools were critical to the execution of the project.

She was in her office talking animatedly on the phone. Her team were in offices around her office. They also seemed to be very busy on their phones. A hardworking group of people.

Madri welcomed Arjuna into her office and bade him sit down. She finished her call and turned to greet him.

"Hi, Arjuna, what brings you here?"

"You know, Madri, I am trying to create a framework for project health assessment."

"Yeah, I know about this."

"At this moment, I am exploring the vital sign 'Execution Excellence,' and I feel that one of the key areas of this would be the timely resourcing of skills and tools. As a new person to the program, I thought this will also help me understand how we do the resourcing for us."

"Okay. Yes. That is correct. Without the right people, tools and environment, it will be difficult to execute any project. Did you want to talk of any particular project?"

"Not really. I suppose what you are doing is germane to all projects within the program?"

"Ah, yes."

Arjuna said, "Tell me, how do you ensure that you have the right resources available for the projects within the program?"

Madri thought for a few minutes and said, "I receive forecasts – some timely, some not so timely – of the requirements from the project managers. Therefore, the pipeline for resource requirements is known somewhat adequately in advance. This makes it easy for me to acquire the required resources."

"Don't all projects send these forecasts as required?"

"Most of them do. But some of them don't. They come and create a scene at the last minute. Of course, I can't blame them. Even they may not know what they want in advance."

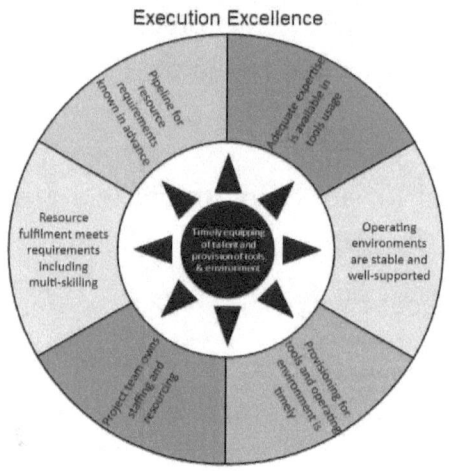

"Are the project teams happy with the way you respond to their resource requirements?"

"Yes. More or less. We try to actually involve the project management team in the staffing and resourcing process. Most of them do feel ownership of this. So, for most projects it is not just passing this to the support functions like ours and blaming them when things do not work out."

Arjuna asked, "Nowadays, access to multi-skilled talent to cope with new technologies and approaches is critical."

"You are right. We participate in project reviews so that we get early heads-up on new technologies and new skill needs. We also get to then think of how effectively multi-skilling can meet some of these requirements."

Arjuna said, "This is good. What about access to technical resources? Are you also not responsible for that?"

"Yes, I am. I liaise with the system resources group to ensure that the project gets access to all environments required for development, testing, UAT, staging, etc."

Madri continued, "We also monitor these environments to ensure that they are stable and always ready for use by the projects. In addition to this, we provide all the required tools required for executing the project."

Arjuna said, "Looks like you have the resources angle under control. Is there any other support you provide?"

"We also resource any expertise needed in the use of tools and the environment."

"Thanks, Madri. I am happy with the support you are providing to the projects in my program."

"Thanks, Arjuna. It was great meeting you."

Arjuna reported back to Krishna and briefed him about his discussion with Madri.

Krishna said, "You seem to have had a good meeting. I think I can summarize the manifestations of the component 'Timely resourcing of talent, tools, environment.' They are:

- Pipeline for resource requirements is known adequately in advance.
- Resource fulfillment meets project requirements including multi-skilling to enable adoption of new technologies and approaches.
- Project ownership of staffing and other resources required for the project.
- Access provisioning to the tools and the operating environment is speedy and well-supported.
- Operating environments are stable and well-supported.
- Adequate expertise is available in appropriate use of tools."

Visibility of Progress Toward Goals, Understanding of Drivers and Course Correction

"Ladies and gentlemen, the Captain has turned on the 'fasten seat belt' sign. If you haven't already done so, please stow your carry-on luggage underneath the seat in front of you or in an overhead bin. Please take your seat and fasten your seat belt. And also make sure your seatback and folding trays are in their full upright position."

Arjuna was on his way to attend a program manager's conclave in Lankanagara far to the south of Hastinapura. He belted himself down as per the request of the flight attendant. He was in a window seat.

The person on his left softly said, "Hi, Arjuna." Only then he looked and saw that the person on his right was one of the staff working on his program.

Arjuna said, "Hi."

The person said, "I am Revati. I work in the Samyojana Project."

Arjuna was thankful that she had identified herself. He did not know her.

"What do you do on the project?"

"I am project admin to Sahadevi and the project."

"Oh, okay."

She said with a smile, "My main job is being progress chaser for Sahadevi."

"Ah!"

Arjuna thought that he could use this opportunity to explore one of the components of Execution Excellence. It was a long flight. Around three hours.

He asked her, "Can we discuss the project for a while, or are you busy with something else?"

"No. I can talk."

"Okay, you know, I have had discussions with Sahadevi, Madri and Damayanti. I am trying to create a framework for assessing the health of projects, and one of the areas I am exploring with your project is Execution Excellence."

"I know. Sahadevi told me."

"It is good that I can pick your brain. Revati, I want to understand from you about project monitoring and reviews. I am sure you have some visibility of this?"

"Yes. I do. I actively support Sahadevi in this area."

Arjuna was happy. He asked, "How does Sahadevi know that the project is progressing satisfactorily?"

She said, "For one thing, there are regular review meetings with all the modules of the project."

"How often?"

"There is a review meeting with each module team every two weeks and a meeting with the team/module leader every week."

"Does she meet only with the team?"

"Well, she also reviews the deliverables every two weeks with the customer."

"Ah, now it becomes interesting. This is critical."

"How often are these meetings held, and what is done at these meetings?"

"Once every two weeks. In these meetings, project progress is tracked against the plan with respect to long and short-term goals."

She continued, "And these meetings are held transparently. These meetings involve key team members so that the customer and the team members get the full picture."

Arjuna asked, "What about any dependencies?"

"All dependencies are tracked and monitored regularly."

Arjuna said, "I meant external dependencies."

Revati asked, "What do you mean?"

"You know, any dependencies outside the project's control."

"For example?"

"Use of a computer resource that belongs to some other department or arrival of the shipment of a component that is needed for testing, etc."

"Oh, I understand. All these external dependencies that are identified in the plan are tracked and monitored in the meetings with the team and module leaders. I also track these separately."

"Okay."

"The other key thing, Arjuna, is that before we accept any resource offer or baselines from external parties, including the customer, we thoroughly validate these with respect to requirements and quality."

"What are these?"

"Examples are preexisting code, preexisting test suite, preexisting architecture, hardware components from external vendors, etc., given to us."

Arjuna said, "All right. This is good. This way the dependencies become more controlled."

"Yes. That is right."

Arjuna said, "Now, one of the key things I think is important is re-planning as needed."

Revati said, "Yes. We do that very religiously. We have set trigger conditions, and if any of these are met, we immediately go into a re-planning cycle."

Arjuna asked, "What are some of the trigger conditions?"

"As examples, three of them are: A change in requirements, missing of internal milestones, joining date of a team member delayed."

"Okay. I get the picture. In addition to re-planning where required, what else happens after reviews?"

"Well, we initiate corrective actions and follow through with them."

"You mean changing the code, design, etc."

Revati said, "Not only that; corrective actions are initiated at all levels of the organization, including at the management level if required."

"Okay. That makes sense."

"Ladies and gentlemen, as we start our descent, please make sure that your tray tables are secured and your seat backs are in their full upright position. Make sure your seat belt is securely fastened and all carry-on luggage is stowed underneath the seat in front of you or in the overhead bins. Thank you."

Arjuna and Revati hastened to comply with the flight attendant's request.

Krishna had also come to Lankanagara to attend the same conference that Arjuna and Revati were going to.

One day after the plenum was over, Krishna and Arjuna met for a drink in the bar in the hotel they were staying in.

Arjuna was in a happy mood. In fact, he was so happy that he had had a drink too many!

Arjuna said, "How is the concave, I mean enclave, I mean conclave going? Anything useful?"

Krishna said, "You know how these conferences are. Only the most dedicated pick up anything useful."

"I liked the discussions on Scrum of Scrums and the role of the Agile Program Manager."

Krishna said, "You are effectively an Agile Program Manager, running many projects. Some may be using Scrum. Others may not."

"I am, aren't I? I hope am an Agile Program Manager in two ways! Where Agile is used as an adjective and where Agile is used as a noun!"

"You are indeed."

"You are great, man. We must do this often."

"Of course, we should. Tell me, have you made any progress in the vital signs discussions?"

"Yes. I have. In fact, on the way in, on the flight, I met Revati. She is the project admin to Sahadevi."

"All right. What did you discuss?"

"We talked about progress monitoring and course correction."

Krishna said, "That is good. In fact, one of the components of Execution Excellence is this: 'Visibility of progress toward goals, understanding of drivers and course correction.'"

Arjuna said, "Yes. That is correct. Progress of visibility... I mean, Visibility of Progress..."

Krishna asked, "What are the manifestations of this?"

Arjuna said, "Revati said that Sahadevi had review meetings with the module teams every other week and module leaders every week. She also meets with the customer for a review every other week. In these meetings, they track and monitor project progress against plans with respect to short and long-term goals."

"Okay. I think we can gather two manifestations from what you are saying."

"What are they?"

"One: Deliverables are reviewed progressively at appropriate periodicity; and two: Project progress is tracked against the plan with respect to short-term and long-term goals."

"Okay. She said that these meetings are held transparently so that the team members know what is going on. So, I can say that a manifestation is: Project progress and reviews are transparent and involve key team members."

Krishna said, "Okay. That is good. What else?"

Arjuna said, "Revati was good. She directly pointed me to another manifestation: External dependencies identified in the plan are monitored on a regular basis."

"Excellent."

Krishna said, "One of the key things in running a project smoothly is to ensure that any code or other things like acceptance test suites given by the customer is validated properly. Otherwise, you may hit bugs and testing problems."

"True. Revati was clear that: Resources/baselines from external sources (customer, partner, sub-contractor, etc.) are validated before acceptance."

"Perfect. What about corrective actions and re-planning when needed?"

"They re-plan when any triggers are hit and take the required corrective actions at all levels."

Krishna asked, "So, can we say that two of the key manifestations are: Project re-planning happens when the trigger conditions are met, and progress review and course correction activities happen at multiple levels in the organization?"

"Yes. Perfect."

"Good, I think you have nailed down another component of the Execution Excellence vital sign. Good work."

"Thank you, Krishna. I will just reiterate these manifestations. They are:

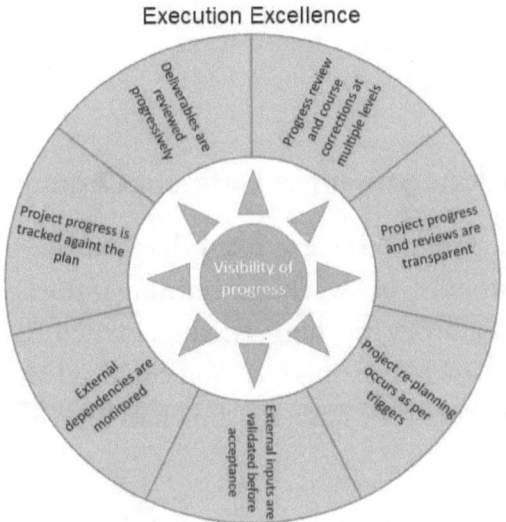

Component:

Visibility of progress toward goals, understanding of drivers and course correction

Manifestations:

- "Deliverables are reviewed progressively at appropriate periodicity.
- Project progress is tracked against the plan with respect to short-term and long-term goals.
- External dependencies identified in the plan are monitored on a regular basis.
- Resources/baselines from external sources (customer, partner, sub-contractor, etc.) are validated before acceptance.
- Project re-planning happens when the trigger conditions are met.
- Project progress and reviews are transparent and involve key team members.

- Progress review and course correction activities happen at multiple levels in the organization."

"Good."

Proactive Risk Management at Different Organization Levels

Krishna was an amateur pilot. He liked flying small planes. This was a hobby that he pursued every weekend morning if the weather conditions were good. That Saturday morning, Krishna invited Arjuna to the flying club airfield just outside Hastinapura. You could get small planes on rent if you were a member of the club. Krishna had been a member for many years now.

That morning, Krishna rented a Cirrus SR22 four-seater plane. And just as dawn broke, they were away. This plane was a single piston-engine aircraft, and Arjuna got a feeling of exhilaration when they lifted off.

They reached their prescribed cruise height of 15000 feet and settled down to a peaceful flight. Arjuna enjoyed the flight a lot. He looked down and saw the Ganges flowing majestically below. When they went east a little, they could also see the Yamuna. There were many cities dotted around. Below was one of the most densely populated areas in the world.

They were in the air for about one hour, and they decided it was time to get back. Arjuna wanted coffee badly.

They were cleared for landing by Hastinapura ATC, and Krishna came down to around 5000 feet when it happened. The engine just stopped. It had failed. Krishna tried all the suggested techniques to bring the engine back to life but failed. They were losing precious time. This aircraft was not a good glider. Arjuna suddenly panicked. They were going to crash!

Suddenly he felt a tug on the aircraft. Krishna motioned him to look up and behind. And that was when he saw the big parachute that had opened. It was connected to the aircraft and was slowing down the descent. The aircraft slowly sank to the ground and settled down in a wheat field near the airstrip. Some of the farmers, who had fled when they saw the plane coming down, now gathered around them. It was an ignominious landing, but they were alive.

Krishna said, "Sorry, Arjuna. The engine just conked out."

"Does this happen often?"

"Not very often."

"Thank God there was a parachute. I never knew that there were parachutes that were attached to the whole plane. I thought parachutes were for individuals."

"Yes. Normally it is. But the Cirrus range of planes are fitted with a Cirrus Airframe Parachute System that has come in handy when planes get into trouble."

"Wow. You learn something new every day."

"Yes."

By this time, rescue workers had arrived from the airfield, and they were taken back to the terminal building.

Over a cup of coffee and a fresh croissant, they got into discussing disasters and risks.

"Whew, that was a narrow escape."

Arjuna said again, "Yes. Thank God for the parachute."

"You must have seen fighter planes deploying parachutes for braking after landing?"

"Yes, that I have seen."

"This parachute that is fitted to the Cirrus plane was developed by a company called BRS."

Arjuna said, "This is very high-level risk management!"

Execution Excellence | 175

"Yes. You know projects and programs also require risk identification and mitigation at various levels."

"You are right. Risk management has to happen at all levels."

Krishna said, "You know, Arjuna, this has to be a component of Execution Excellence. 'Proactive risk management at different organization levels.'"

"That is correct. A project without risk management will not be inherently healthy on a sustained basis."

"Yes. What would be the manifestations of this component?"

"To understand that, let us look at airplane safety. An airplane can face risks at a personal level – pilot falling sick, pilot drunk, pilot drowsy, etc., etc.; at the aircraft level – engine failure, structural failure, avionics failure, control surface failures, etc., etc.; at the environment level – weather conditions, landing terrain conditions, etc.; and also at the external conditions level – stress of pilot, pressure to get to a place fast, etc."

Krishna continued, "Similarly, the project needs to identify risks with respect to people, operating environment, tools, data, suppliers, components, product requirements, architecture and process, etc., and figure out avoidance and/or mitigation strategies for each risk."

Arjuna said, "Yes, I agree. This must be done for each project."

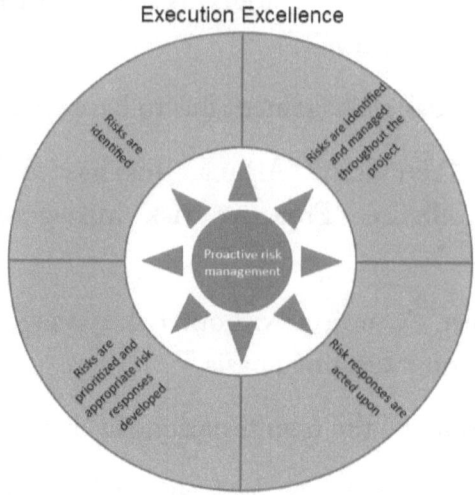

Krishna said, "And risks have to be prioritized based on the conditions the project is in, and right mitigation actions need to be implemented."

Arjuna said, "That is true. The parachute that saved us today may have been a problem on a very windy day."

"Yes. That is correct. We should prioritize project risk based on their impact on the goals."

Krishna continued. "And remember, risks need to be identified and managed throughout the project cycle. The pilot of the plane must constantly monitor the situation and prioritize the risk and make plans to deploy the right management plan."

"Thank you, Krishna. I think I now have a good idea of the component and its manifestations. Let me recap them here:

Component:

Proactive risk management at different organization levels

Manifestations:

- "Risks are identified with respect to people, operating environment, tools, data, suppliers, components, product requirements, architecture and process.
- Risks are prioritized and managed for mitigation of their impact on the project goals.
- Risk responses are acted upon in project planning and execution.
- Risks are identified and managed throughout the lifecycle of the project."

Project Budget and Tracking

Arjuna was having some water at the water cooler when Krishna walked by.

"How's it going, Arjuna?"

"Well, I am trying to put together all the components of the vital sign Execution Excellence. I think we have got them all covered."

Krishna said, "There is one more area that you have to look at to ensure Execution Excellence."

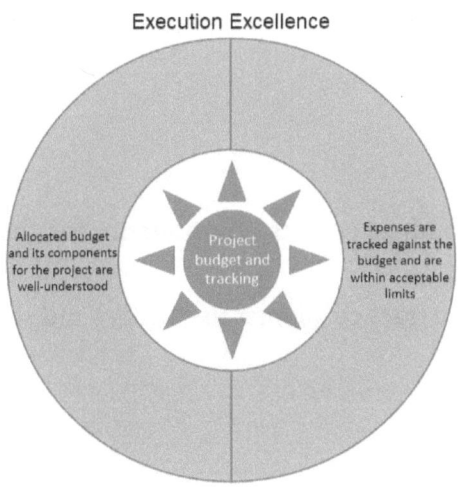

"What is it?"

"Budgeting. A healthy project will have effective project budgeting and tracking."

He continued, "A project's allocated budgets and its component need to be well understood by all concerned."

"What are the things that need to be tracked?"

Krishna said, "For example, Travel, Hardware, Training, Investment, Contingency and People Cost."

Arjuna said, "And, of course, one needs to track one's project ongoing cost against the approved budget and take corrective/preventive actions when the actuals significantly vary compared to the budget (at that stage)."

"Exactly."

"Anything else on budgets and tracking of them?"

"No, this is it."

"Let me summarize:

Component:

Project budget and tracking

Manifestations:

- Allocated budget and its components for the project are well-understood.
- Expenses are tracked against the budget and are within acceptable limits."

"Excellent."

Summarizing Execution Excellence

When Krishna and Arjuna presented Yudhishthira their conclusions about Execution Excellence, he was very impressed. He said, "You are making good progress, I see."

Components	Manifestations
Clarity of project goals and success criteria – short-term and long-term	Project's purpose and Business Case are well documented and available for the team
	Customer milestones (short-term and long-term) are well-understood
	There is common understanding between the customer and the team on the definition of deliverables for each milestone
	There is recognition for meeting the goals successfully
	Impact on stakeholders of failure to meet goals is well understood by the team
Estimates reflect capability to deliver	Inputs to estimation include functional & non-functional requirements, and it is done by people with the required expertise
	Size is estimated based on the product scope and the nature of work
	Effort, cost and duration are derived from size with appropriate considerations for product attributes, platform attributes, tools used and people capability

Components	Manifestations
	Past data from the project and the organization are used appropriately to derive predictable estimates
	Estimates are realistic
	Estimation assumptions are documented and tracked throughout the project for appropriate actions if they turn out to be false
	Estimates are agreed upon among stakeholders as appropriate and are used to validate ability to deliver on the commitments
Adaptive integrated plans	Plans exist to address requirements and project goals
	Plans have resilience to meet project goals within tolerance levels
	Internal milestones are well-defined and granular to meet short-term customer milestones
	Progressive elaboration of activities is practiced and is accepted by stakeholders
	Project plans identify dependencies (upstream & downstream) and are shared with appropriate stakeholders
	Project plans include review points for progress assessment
	Project plan provides for review of deliverables

Components	Manifestations
	Trigger conditions are identified which require re-planning
	Plans are revised when risks materialize or when unforeseen events occur
	Planning and tracking are well-supported through the right tools
	Plans are independently reviewed initially and when significant changes occur
	Plans are adapted to incorporate new technologies and approaches and the required multi-skilling
Timely resourcing of talent, tools, environment	Pipeline for resource requirements is known adequately in advance
	Resource fulfillment meets project requirements
	Project ownership of staffing and other resources required for the project
	Provisioning for the tools and the operating environment is speedy and well-supported
	Operating environments are stable and well-supported
	Adequate expertise is available in appropriate use of tools
	Resource fulfillment meets project requirements including multi-skilling to enable adoption of new technologies and approaches

Components	Manifestations
Visibility of progress toward goals, understanding of drivers and course correction	Deliverables are reviewed progressively at appropriate periodicity
	Project progress is tracked against the plan with respect to short-term and long-term goals
	External dependencies identified in the plan are monitored on a regular basis
	Resources/baselines from external sources (customer, partner, sub-contractor, etc.) are validated before acceptance
	Project re-planning occurs when the trigger conditions are met
	Project progress and reviews are transparent and involve key team members
	Progress review and course correction activities happen at multiple levels in the organization
Proactive risk management at different organization levels	Risks are identified with respect to risk sources applicable to the project (such as product requirements, scope, people, resources, assumptions, dependencies, etc.)
	Risks are prioritized and appropriate risk responses developed
	Risk responses are acted upon in project planning and execution
	Risks are identified and managed throughout the lifecycle of the project

Components	Manifestations
Project budget and tracking	Allocated budget and its components for the project are well-understood
	Expenses are tracked against the budget and are within acceptable limits

Chapter 6

Engaged Management

A crisis!

Arjuna was woken up in the middle of the night by a phone call from the office. There was a crisis. A few of the testers of project Indravyuha within the Kurukshetra umbrella had stayed behind at night to test a critical part of their project. The Indravyuha Project was key to the defense of Hastinapura. The project developed some of the key algorithms for guiding the so-called "National" missiles that intercepted and destroyed any oncoming hostile missiles and planes into the city. There were more than two hundred engineers working on this development.

The testing platform had a bank of high-speed computers and disk units. One of these disk units had disappeared! The testing platform was no longer functional.

The project manager of Indravyuha, Yayati, was panicking. He was almost incoherent when he called Arjuna at night to report the problem.

Yayati was shouting, "The disk unit is gone. It was there when we came in this morning. We had made sure that the platform was working."

Arjuna asked, "Why were you working at night?"

"Well, the test plans call for very high CPU and network usage. We thought that if we worked at night we could get near exclusive use of these."

"Okay, who have you informed about this?"

"Only you."

"I will be there soon. Meanwhile, make sure all of you stay there. Nobody should leave."

Arjuna was very concerned. He knew that Yayati had not realized the gravity of the problem. There were two issues here. One was that the testing platform was not functional. The second was that the missing disk unit may have contained some critical and sensitive data.

First of all, he called the corporate security group and informed them of the problem. They promised that they would constitute a team straightway to look into this. He then called Yudhishthira and apprised him of the situation.

Yudhishthira said, "Arjuna. Don't worry. Things will turn out all right."

Arjuna immediately started for office.

About half an hour later, four of them met in Yudhishthira's office – Yudhishthira himself, Arjuna, Yayati and Urvashi, the head of corporate security.

Yudhishthira opened the conversation. He said, "Yayati, tell us exactly what has happened. You can be assured that there will be no witch hunt to pin the blame on anyone."

Yayati looked worried. He said, "Well, we planned to stay back at night so that we could get uninterrupted time on the central computers and the network, so that we could test our algorithms. The testing team of five engineers, myself and two of the developers stayed behind. Things were going well. We ran a few of the preliminary tests and then went to have our dinner in the cafeteria. We were away for about half an hour. When we came back, we found that the platform was not working. We checked and found that one of the disk units was missing."

Urvashi asked, "The computer center people will know what happened, won't they?"

Yayati said, "No. It was our local test center."

Arjuna hastened to explain, "Some of the projects, especially the ones developing intricate algorithms, have their own testing centers. These centers normally host the machines required for the test platforms and are completely under the projects. Yayati is talking about a disk unit missing from the testing center attached to his project."

"So, the central computer center people have no knowledge of what goes on here?"

"No."

Urvashi was not a technical person. She asked, "What is the real issue? What is the damage?"

Yudhishthira said, "There are two issues. One falls under your purview and is very critical. The other is an internal matter of my department. The first issue, which falls under your purview, is that the disk unit may contain sensitive data about the city's defenses. Some data of this nature was loaded into the disk to make the tests as real as possible. It will be very bad for us if the data got into the wrong hands."

Urvashi said, "I understand. And, for my knowledge, what is the second issue?"

"It is the issue of service continuity. We need to make sure that we can recover quickly from this and continue our test."

"Okay, I suppose you will be looking into that separately? I will concentrate on the missing unit."

She asked Yayati, "Who is in charge of the test center?"

"One of the test engineers."

"Who will have the knowledge to pull out a memory unit from the configuration?"

"All the test engineers have this knowledge. Anyway, there is no skill required to pull out the disk unit."

"Who is privy to the knowledge of what data is stored in these disk units?"

Yayati said, "All the test engineers and myself. And to some extent Arjuna and the customer representative for this project."

"Have you informed the customer of this problem?"

"Not yet."

"Was anybody from the customer team here today?"

"No."

"Okay, let us get to some details now. You say that when you went for dinner, the testing platform was functioning well?"

"Yes. That is right. We did some pre-tests on the platform, and they went well."

"Who all went to dinner?"

"All of us."

"Meaning?"

"Myself, two developers and five testing engineers."

"Did anybody come back to the testing center during the meal?"

"No. Nobody did."

"Let me reframe the question. Did anybody leave the table during the meal?"

"Not that I remember."

"Was there anybody in the testing center when you left for dinner?"

"Nobody. All of us went for dinner."

"Okay. Can you call your senior-most test engineer here? I would like to talk to him."

"I will send her in. Should I also come in with her?"

"No. You needn't."

Yayati almost looked relieved when he went out. Soon, Tilottama, the lead test engineer for the project Indravyuha, came in.

Urvashi asked her, "Tilottama, you understand the gravity of the situation we are in, don't you?"

"Yes, I do." She seemed to be more composed than Yayati.

Urvashi asked, "When you went for dinner, was there anyone in the testing center?"

Tilottama said, "Yes. The janitor was here."

"I see, now we are getting somewhere. Was he the normal janitor that comes to clean the center?"

"I have stayed back a few times at night. The janitor who comes in normally is a lady. This was a man. I have never seen him before."

"Did all of you go for dinner together?"

"Yes."

"Who all?"

"Myself, Yayati, two of the developers and four testing engineers in my team."

"When you were eating, did anybody leave the table for anything?"

"Well, Yayati got a phone call, and he left the table to talk. However, he did not stay long. His call was short. He walked to the end of the room and came back. One of the test engineers also got a call. He went outside the cafeteria to take the call. He must have been away for about ten minutes."

"For the record, is this ten minutes time enough to go to the test center and rip out the disk unit?"

"More than time enough."

"Okay, that is all."

When Tilottama left them, Urvashi said, "This is the problem with people. When we asked Yayati, he said that that there was no one in the center when they went for dinner. His mind was full of engineers. It did not occur to him that he had to mention the janitor. What he meant

Engaged Management | 191

was that there were no engineers or managers. The janitor was not in his reckoning. Similarly, when he said nobody left during dinner, he meant nobody left the dinner early to go back. He did not think of the engineer leaving for ten minutes as 'leaving,' or his own leaving to take the phone call."

She continued, "But this lady Tilottama is smart. She was very clear on this. For the sake of cross-checking, we should ask one more engineer about this."

They called in another testing engineer of the group. He was between Yayati and Tilottama in remembering details.

Urvashi asked him, "After dinner, did you directly come back?"

"No. We stopped at the ice cream stall for an ice cream."

"All of you?"

"Now that you mention it, Tilottama did not have an ice cream. She hurried down since she had to do something. In fact, it was she who discovered that the disk unit was missing."

Urvashi said, "This is interesting. So, she came back before you all did. How many minutes after her did you all come down?"

"About five minutes. We did not finish our ice creams in the cafeteria. We brought them down after a while."

"When you came down, was the janitor still there?"

"No, he had gone."

Urvashi said, "I will now go back to my office and do some investigation. Let me look at the output from the CCTV cameras. I am not sure that it can tell us anything, since the cameras are only outside the space with the office, against the door that leads to the lifts and staircase. Our HR policy does not allow us to have cameras inside. I will go back and ask the security people also."

When Urvashi left, Yudhishthira turned to Arjuna. "Well, what do you think?"

"My worry is about the data being compromised. I hope that we can recover the disk soon."

Yudhishthira said, "Urvashi will recover the disk and also find the criminal who did this. She and her team are very good and experienced at this. Do you have any guesses as to who could have done this?"

"I think it is the janitor. He was new. When he saw the blinking lights of the disks, he could not resist pulling one out. Or maybe someone from outside came in and did the job?"

"You may be right. But, I don't think it is the janitor. Anyway, let us wait till Urvashi completes her investigation."

Arjuna said, "Yudhishthira, why don't you go home? I will stay back and keep you updated on any developments with Urvashi. I will work with the team and see how we can get the test platform up and running."

"Okay. I will see you tomorrow."

When they met the next day, Yudhishthira asked Arjuna, "What have you learned from this episode about the health of projects?"

"I think it is about management support for projects. Your coming down here immediately to support us and help us has buoyed up mine as well as Yayati's spirits."

Yudhishthira said, "I agree with you. A management that is engaged with the projects is required to ensure the success of any project. Of course, management is duty-bound to address a crisis like this."

Arjuna said, "Yes. You are right. I will talk to Krishna on this."

"Okay, that will be good."

Crisis Resolved

Arjuna went to the project floor and met with Yayati. He wanted to know what steps were being taken by Yayati to restore the testing platform so that the work could continue.

Yayati said, "I think we can recover the test platform. We have a spare disk unit. We can restore the data on the disk from the backup we took last week. This disk unit did not contain any data that was being modified. It only had input data. Tilottama is working at loading this data from the backup unit on to the disk."

"How long will it take to recover the disk and to start the testing again?"

"About eight hours."

"Did we not commit to the customer that we will demonstrate this algorithm today? Can we meet this deadline now?"

"No, we cannot. But, we can demonstrate it tomorrow. We are only a day late."

"That is not good."

"I know, but what can we do? I didn't think that somebody would rip off a disk unit."

Arjuna said, "Well, now we know we need to be prepared for these eventualities also. This is one of the uncertainties of a project."

He continued, "I will talk to my counterpart at the customer's and update him on this first thing in the morning. You can talk to your counterpart after that."

"Okay."

Arjuna went back to his office and sent a message to Yudhishthira on the plans to restore the platform for use. Then he waited.

About an hour later, Urvashi walked into his room.

She said, "You are not going to like what I am about to tell you."

Arjuna braced himself for the bad news.

Urvashi said, "Well, we are sure that the janitor did not take the disk unit. For one, he may not have the technical knowledge to pull out the disk unit without damaging it and the backplane. I looked at the backplane. It was not damaged. The disk seems to have been disconnected by a person who knew what to do. Secondly, we looked at the video of the janitor going out. He did not carry anything out with him."

She continued, "The engineer who spent ten minutes away from the table to take the phone call did not come down to the testing project room. He just stood outside the cafeteria to take his call. The video recordings confirm that."

"Tilottama did not stay back to have an ice cream. She hurried down to the project floor. When she came in, she thought that she was alone. However, the janitor was still there. He was doing some cleaning under a table. The janitor says that he saw her going quickly to the 'computer room' and coming out almost immediately with what he thought was a video player in her hand."

Arjuna asked, "Where did she hide it?"

"It must be somewhere in the project floor. She did not have the time to take it out or even take any data out."

"What do we do now?"

"Well, you must immediately ask her to leave the project floor and tell her that she is suspended from the project till the investigations are complete. I am pretty sure that she is the culprit. If that is the case, we will need to dismiss her and file a police case against her. The charges against her may be very serious since she will be accused of trying to steal classified defense data. They may not move against her till she names the people she was working with. It may be a foreign power. She may be an unwitting tool."

Arjuna's head spun. One of his own team members! Arjuna immediately informed Yudhishthira about this development. He agreed with Urvashi's suggestions.

Arjuna went down to the project floor and met Yayati and told him the situation. Yayati went into shock! Arjuna knew that he could not count on Yayati to fire Tilottama. He had to do it himself.

Yayati said, "Thank you, Arjuna. Your support has been very valuable. I do not know what I would have done if you had started laying blame on me or any of the others."

Arjuna thought, "I am 'management' for Yayati and the team!"

Tilottama and a couple of the testing engineers were trying to restore the data from the backup unit.

Arjuna called Tilottama out and told her that she was a suspect in the case of the missing disk unit and she had to leave the project floor immediately and she should not come back to the project till she was called back.

Surprisingly, her protest was very muted. She must have known that the game was up. When she was leaving, she was accosted by Urvashi and a couple of her officers…

Arjuna then asked the two engineers to continue the work of restoring the data.

About an hour later, Urvashi came to Arjuna's office. She had the missing unit with her. She said that she was pretty sure that the data had not been compromised. Tilottama did not have the time or opportunity to send any data out. She had hidden the disk unit in the dustbin inside the ladies' toilet. Since the janitor had come and gone, she was sure that the dustbin would not be emptied till the next day.

The crisis was thus resolved within a few hours. The disk unit, thanks to Tilottama's correct handling when taking it out, could be slotted back in and the platform was as good and as ready to go. The customer deadline could still be met!

By the next day, it was established that Tilottama had indeed been the culprit. She confessed that someone had approached her with the promise of a lot of money. She was going through a bad financial patch and felt that the money would help her out of the crisis. Arjuna and Yudhishthira felt that sacking her from her job was punishment enough, but the corporate security people felt that an example had to be made of her and so filed a police complaint.

Tilottama was arrested but was able to get bail. The trial would take its own course...

Yudhishthira confidentially told Arjuna, "If you repeat what I am about to tell you to anyone, I will deny I said it. I will not be surprised if we find that that crook Shakuni from the Kauravas had a hand in this…"

Arjuna did not comment.

Arjuna went in search of Krishna as soon as he reached the office the next morning. He gave Krishna a summary of the events relating to the loss of the disk unit and its recovery and the arrest of Tilottama.

Krishna said, "Poor lady. She must have been going through a bad patch. You know, sometimes, we don't realize the difficulties other people are going through. And there are people waiting out there to take advantage of people's difficulties. Corruption starts like this. Once you fall into the hands of one of these manipulators, there is no easy way out. Once you do a corrupt or illegal act, they have you where they want you. They can then start blackmailing you."

Arjuna felt sorry for Tilottama.

He gave Krishna a brief about his discussions with Yudhishthira on the vital sign of management support.

Krishna said, "Good. I think the next vital sign we need to nail down is 'Engaged Management.'"

"Engaged Management?"

"Yes. This is what we want, a management that is fully engaged with the ups and downs of a project."

Management Takes Action to Remove Impediments and Provide Resources

Arjuna said, "Why don't we have a discussion with Yayati and ask him what kind of expectations he has from an 'Engaged Management?'"

"Okay."

They went in search of Yayati. He was still recovering from the trauma he went through with the loss of the disk unit and the arrest of Tilottama.

Arjuna asked, "Yayati, how are you?"

"I am well. Am still reeling under the events leading to Tilottama's arrest."

"Yes. It must have been a traumatic experience for you, to know that the disk unit was gone."

"Yes. I am still shivering."

Arjuna said, "Tell me, Yayati, what was your overall impression of the support you got from management on this?"

"What do you mean by 'management?'"

"People who are supervising you, people who provide support from outside, etc."

"Like you, Yudhishthira, Urvashi etc.?"

"Exactly."

Yayati said, "I found management support extremely good. In fact, without the support I received from you and Yudhishthira, I would not have been able to handle the theft situation."

"What in your mind is the most important feature of this management support?"

"The main feature is the ability to escalate issues to management in a timely manner, like I was able to do the night before."

"Okay. I suppose this impressed you, didn't it?"

"Yes."

"What else?"

"The other thing is the lack of hesitation in the management group to commit resources and funds to removing any impediments."

Krishna said, "Yes. This is important. If Urvashi and others had not stepped in right away, the cause would have been lost. And the important thing is to ensure that any impediments are removed in a systemic manner rather than as just a one-off thing."

Yayati said, "Exactly."

Arjuna sked, "What else would you say is important?"

"There are two other important things in my mind. One is that you and Yudhishthira consult us before making commitments to the customer."

"Okay, what is the other?"

"Your experience should guide us on reviews of the project and help us course-correct."

"I get it. Thanks, Yayati. I will be talking to some of your team members and the customer also to understand the efficacy of management engagement in the project."

Arjuna and Krishna went back to Krishna's office.

Krishna said, "That was a good chat with Yayati."

"Yes. It was. We got some idea of one component of the vital sign 'Engaged Management.'"

Krishna said, "Do you recall the incident with Bhanumati, who came running to you with a problem of continually changing requirements from customer?"

"Yes. Of course, we got the customer to agree to the transitioning of the project to use an Agile approach."

"This was a good example of Engaged Management. You kept the team away from this issue and came up with a solution that the team can implement. This falls into the same component as the issue you discussed with Yayati."

Arjuna asked, "What can we call the component?"

"Can we call it, 'Management takes action to remove impediments and provide resources?'"

"Okay. This makes sense."

"Can you summarize the manifestations of this component?"

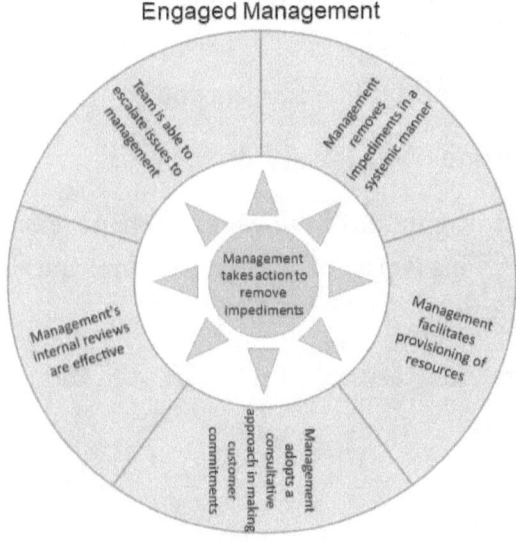

"Okay. Here it is:

Component:

Management takes action to remove impediments and provide resources

Manifestations:

- Team is able to escalate issues to management in a timely manner.

- Management's internal reviews of the project are effective.
- Management adopts a consultative approach in making customer commitments.
- Management facilitates provisioning of the necessary resources including funds for timely and speedy removal of impediments.
- Management removes impediments in a systemic manner (as opposed to just addressing it as a transaction).

Management Involvement in Project and Interest in the Team

Arjuna walked onto the floor where the Indravyuha engineers were hard at work. He had fixed a meeting with one of the engineers, Hidimbi. She was waiting for him.

Arjuna said, "Hi, Hidimbi. How are you?"

"I am good, Arjuna. What can I do for you?"

"I am trying to figure out how well our management engages with the project teams. This is part of my research into the six vital signs that indicate project health."

"By management, I assume you mean you and Yudhishthira and others of that rank?"

"Yes."

Hidimbi said, "Well, I think there is adequate interest shown by management in the interests of the team."

"What do you mean by that?"

"For example, the other day, our team organized a team lunch. You remember that, don't you? We were pleasantly surprised when Yudhishthira himself joined us for lunch that day. His participating in our team's activities raised our spirits quite high."

"Okay. What else do you think is important?"

"However, sometimes I feel that you and Yudhishthira do not understand the team's challenges."

Arjuna was shocked. He thought that he was doing a good job with the teams!

"What do you mean?" Arjuna immediately regretted the curtness of the question.

"Well, I feel that our management doesn't seem to understand women's issues and challenges well."

Arjuna said, "I am sorry about that. We will certainly look into this and ensure that there will be no such problem in the future."

"Don't get me wrong. Things are not all bad. The issue is that the team is mainly men. And on the average, the team interests are well taken care of. But, for us women in the team, there are certain challenges."

"I will discuss with the HR people and also Draupadi to see how we can put in place ways to ensure that these issues don't crop up."

Hidimbi said, "One of the areas where this shows up is when some problems arise with the software or when the customer wants something quickly. In the hurry to satisfy the customer's requirements, you may overlook some of the interests of, especially, women of the team."

"You are saying that there sometimes is no effort to find a balance between people's interest and the interest of the other stakeholders."

"Yes. You need to foster an environment where there is this balance."

"Thank you, Hidimbi, it was an eye-opener talking to you. I am sorry that there had been some issues in the past. We will ensure that this does not happen going forward."

"Thanks, Arjuna. Am ready to help whenever you need me."

Arjuna walked away, humbled.

He straightaway went to Yudhishthira's office and told him about what he learned from Hidimbi. Yudhishthira was concerned.

"There may be other projects too having a similar issue. It was only that Hidimbi was open enough and felt confident enough to talk about it. It is all kudos to you that people feel that they can openly talk to you."

"How shall we tackle this?"

"I will talk to the HR head, Anshuman, and have him do a small inquiry into this and put together a plan to ensure that this issue is taken care of. I will also talk to Draupadi."

"Great. Thanks, Yudhishthira."

When Arjuna met Krishna next, he was feeling a bit down that the Pandava workplace and his program were not very gender-friendly. Sometimes you learn about things that you thought were under control, but really were not.

Krishna said, "Don't worry about this. I have coached so many people like you. Normally, people respond negatively to such inputs. But you have responded positively. You have started putting in place processes to make sure that the issues she raised are addressed."

Krishna continued. "Anyway, the main thing is what you learned from this. What is the component of Engaged Management that you have unearthed in your discussions with Hidimbi?"

"I think the component is about the management's interest in the team."

"Okay, what about the manifestations?"

"Understanding the team's challenges, balancing team's interest with other stakeholders' interests, and fostering an environment that encourages this should be another."

"In fact, it should be split into three manifestations. What about the others?"

"The other main thing is management taking part in the team's activities."

"Good. Can you summarize?"

Component:

Management involvement in project and interest in the team

Manifestations:

- Management fosters a project environment that balances task orientation and people orientation.
- Management takes an active interest in the project and understands the team's challenges.
- Management is effective in addressing project issues, balancing stakeholder needs and adopting a facilitative approach.
- Management participates in team activities as required.

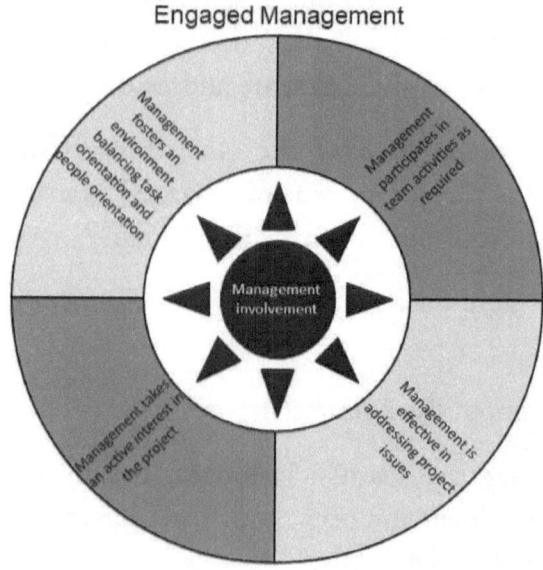

Customer Connection and Insights and Brand Building

Arjuna was at home. His brother-in-law, Drishtadyumna, was visiting, and they were having a great time. There were also a few other guests. A few beers and a good dinner were rounding off the evening.

Drishtadyumna was the marketing manager of a large chip manufacturing company. Their customers were computer manufacturing companies, mobile manufacturers, specialized equipment manufacturers and such.

He was telling the assembled guests about his current efforts to build the brand of his company and a new product of theirs with a large computer manufacturer.

He said, "One of the key things we find that works is that our organization is engaged with the customer at the CEO level, at the VP levels, at the director levels and at the engineering levels. Our CEO talks to their CEO, our VP talks to their VP, etc."

Arjuna asked, "What do they talk about in these discussions?"

"Well, these discussions are used to bring awareness of what we do, our products and also about our efforts at one important project that we are specially undertaking for them – a special chip for one of their computer lines."

Arjuna asked, "Oh, you are custom-making something for them?"

"Yes. Much like what you are doing for the defense department."

"Right. How useful are these meetings?"

"Very useful. At these meetings, our people gather suggestions from the customer and also look for any unsaid intent or requirements."

"These insights can be very valuable."

"Of course. These occasions are also used to represent our organization and our project team to them."

"How often do you do this?"

"We do this on a sustained basis, so that the message is clear and not forgotten."

"This is very interesting. This way, the organizational and the team brand is built and sustained with the customer?"

"Yes. And the meetings at the various levels happen at both formal and informal settings."

Arjuna was impressed. He realized that this was one of the things that he had to do for his team with his customer.

Arjuna met Krishna the next day to discuss this. He summarized what he had learned from Drishtadyumna the previous evening.

Arjuna asked Krishna, "Krishna, what is the management's role in front of the customer as far as a project is concerned?"

"Exactly what you learned from your brother-in-law last evening. Can you distill out a component from your discussions with Drishtadyumna?"

Arjuna said, "In fact, I think I can get two components for the vital sign 'Engaged Management.' 1. Management connects with customer management and brings insight to the team and 2. Management sets, promotes and supports the project team brand."

"Okay. This is starting to look good. What would the manifestations be?"

Arjuna said, "It is very simple, I think. In fact, let me note down the manifestations of the component 'Management connects with customer management and brings insight to the team.'"

"Okay, what are they?"

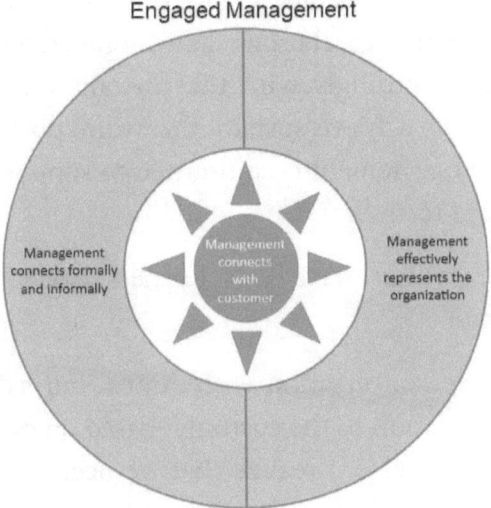

"One: Management connects formally and informally with the customer management at all levels and Two: Management effectively represents the organization and project interests in interactions with the customer."

Krishna said, "Good. And the manifestations of 'Management sets, promotes and supports the project team brand' are…"

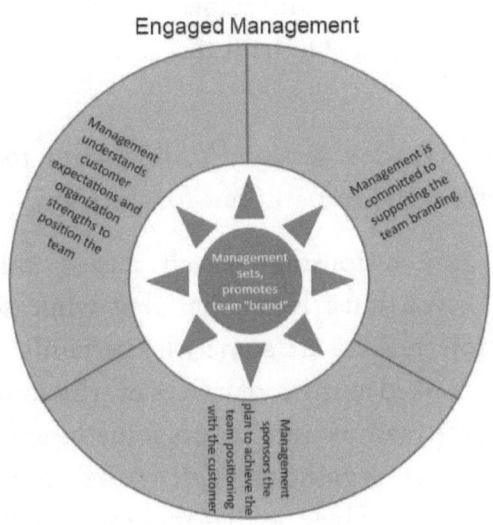

Engaged Management | 209

Arjuna said, "What are its manifestations? One: Management understands customer expectations and organization's strengths to position the team accordingly with the customer; Two: Management sponsors the plan to achieve/sustain the team positioning with the customer; Three: Management is committed to supporting the building & sustenance of the team brand."

Krishna said, "What have you learned from your discussions regarding branding?"

"I remember the conversation with Amba, our sales manager. We have sold our organization to the customer based on our 'brand,' namely, expertise in defense shields. I realize that we need to do everything in our power to live up to it. I have already spoken to the team on this, and we are working out ways and means of achieving it."

Management Enables the Team to Perform at a Higher Level

Yayati had organized a 'project day' of the Indravyuha Project. It was to happen in one of the resorts near their office. Arjuna and Yudhishthira were also invited.

Yayati had organized many games and other fun activities. There was also an uplifting talk on 'Mindfulness' by one of the experts in this area, a Vishweshwar Hegde. He held this project team audience spellbound for two hours.

At the end of Hegde's session, Yudhishthira took the stage to announce a few prizes and recognitions for the team.

Yudhishthira gave a rousing speech during this occasion. He concluded with, "…you must remember that while some people did very well in the project, there are some who certainly need to improve. However, when we looked at the root causes of why some people did not meet expectations, the reasons were always something other than skill or dedication. One person was going through a bad divorce; one person had lost his mother. So, I firmly believe that these so-called failures are very temporary, and moving forward, these very same people can become the stars of the project."

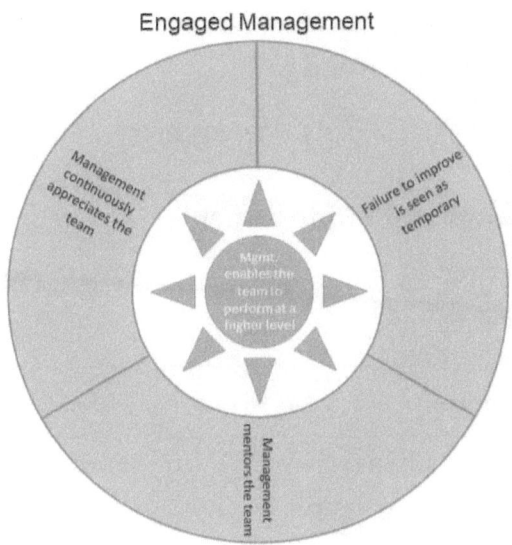

He continued, "We have a set of coaches who can at various levels coach and mentor team members who need support over and above what their supervisors can give them. Also, my door and Arjuna's door and also the doors of the HR team are always open for you. Come and talk to us if you need us. Let me end this talk by recognizing some of the key performers in this project. Achievers who are being recognized today must remember not to rest on their laurels. They must continuously strive to reach higher levels of performance. Now, Subhadra, for her excellent performance in convincing the customer that…"

It was a great speech. Arjuna and Krishna were impressed.

Krishna asked Arjuna, "Now you know the next component of 'Engaged Management.'"

Arjuna said, "Is it Management enables the team to perform at a higher level?"

"Yes. And what are the manifestations?"

"One: Management continuously appreciates the team for their performance while pointing to possibilities for higher performance; Two: Management mentors the team for higher level of performance; Three: Failure to improve is seen as temporary and leadership encourages the team to learn and move forward."

"Okay. That's it for 'Engaged Management.'"

Summarizing Engaged Management

Yudhishthira said, "This brings out clearly the role of management in projects. You have captured this well."

Components	Manifestations
Management takes action to remove impediments and provide resources	Team members are able to escalate issues to management in a timely manner
	Management's internal reviews of the project are effective
	Management adopts a consultative approach in making customer commitments
	Management facilitates provisioning of necessary resources including funds for timely and speedy removal of impediments
	Management removes impediments in systemic manner (as opposed to just addressing it as a transaction)

Components	Manifestations
Management involvement in project and interest in the team	Management fosters a project environment that balances task orientation and people orientation
	Management takes an active interest in the project and understands the team's challenges
	Management is effective in addressing project issues balancing stakeholder needs and adopts a facilitative approach
	Management participates in team activities as required
Management connects with customer management and brings insight to the team	Management connects formally and informally with the customer management at all levels
	Management effectively represents the organization and project interests in interactions with the customer
Management sets, promotes and supports the team "brand"	Management understands customer expectations and organization's strengths to position the team accordingly with the customer
	Management sponsors the plan to achieve and sustain the team positioning with the customer
	Management is committed to supporting the building and sustenance of the team brand

Components	Manifestations
Management enables the team to perform at a higher level	Management continuously appreciates the team for their performance while pointing to possibilities for higher performance

Management mentors the team for higher level of performance

Failure to improve is seen as temporary, and leadership encourages the team to learn and move forward |

Chapter 7
Continuous Improvement

Arjuna was relaxing at home. He had some soft, relaxing music on. He was in a reflective mood. He was thinking of a Zen koan. "Shuzan held out a short stick and said, 'If you call this a short stick, you oppose its reality. If you do not call it a short stick, you ignore the fact. Now what do you wish to call this?'"

What indeed?

One of the main inputs you get from Zen or Dhyana is that you miss seeing the point if you classify or define boundaries for things…

Arjuna, though thinking of meditation, let his mind wander. His mind slipped from Zen to Kaizen or "change for the better." Or improvement.

He was woken up from his reverie by the doorbell ringing. It was his friend Vaishampayana!

"You look like you have seen a ghost!"

"Oh, I was daydreaming."

"Who about? Anyone I know?"

"No. I was daydreaming about Zen and improvement."

"Tell me. This is what I am grappling with on a regular basis. My vendor has no concept of improvement, though 'Continuous Improvement' is one of their objectives!"

Vaishampayana was the General Manager of the marketing division of a retail product company. At this moment, he was neck-deep in the development of a data mining tool for analyzing their customer behavior so that they could look at innovative ways to market their products. He did not seem to be happy with the customer's Continuous Improvement processes.

Arjuna put himself in the vendor's shoes. Though he did not admit it, he too was not sure whether his program was built for Continuous Improvement!

He asked, "Vaishampayana, what do you understand by Continuous Improvement by your vendor?"

Vaishampayana said, "It is really continual improvement, though it is called Continuous Improvement."

"What do you mean?"

"Look, nobody really is looking for an improvement of 0.0001% improvement in something. But, let us say, a new technology comes along and the vendor adopts it, thereby getting an improvement in the code turnaround of, say, 5%. This then is something to write home about. Similarly, a different process comes along which when adopted improves performance by 8%… You get what I mean, right?"

"I think."

"Of course, all improvements cannot be breakthrough improvement. They are incremental. But it is always in spurts."

He continued, "A vendor should always be reflecting of the processes and technologies he is currently implementing and identify sub-optimal items (both against itself and better options available). These can then be improved. A vendor should also be reflecting on the improvement needs of the customer."

Arjuna asked, "What is the customer's role in this?"

"Well, I think the customer should be working with the vendor team to identify Continuous Improvement ideas – technology, approaches, etc., and helping to prioritize and plan these."

Vaishampayana continued, "The customer should also be giving feedback to the vendor team about the results of the improvements."

He also said, "Of course, the customer should be continuously encouraging the team in this area."

"Have you been doing this with your vendor?"

"We have been trying to!"

He continued, "Arjuna, you realize that for this to work, the vendor's management also should be doing the same things with the team as the customer?"

Arjuna thought. "Yes. I suppose you are right. What can I get you? A coffee? A beer?"

When going to meet Krishna the next day, his mind was in a whirl. He was thinking.

Improvement is not something that you can have enough of. Nothing has improved enough. There is always scope for further improvement.

This is why it is called Continuous Improvement (technically, continual improvement). Continuous Improvement is based on a cycle of feedback and acting on that feedback.

If a project is not improving continuously over its lifetime, it is not healthy. Continuous Improvement is surely a vital sign of a project. Do the projects under the Kurukshetra Program have the ability to continuously improve built in?

This is the question that he posed to Krishna after updating him on his discussions with Vaishampayana.

Krishna said, "Improvement imperatives come from two sources; from within the organization and from outside. We need to look at both."

Arjuna asked, "By inside, you mean from team members and from management, and by outside, you mean customers?"

Krishna said, "I meant more than that, but I think for this exercise, we can limit the sources to these you mentioned."

Arjuna said, "Okay."

Krishna said, "Improvement should happen as the team's response to customer expectations or organizational expectations and also as proactive measures from the team, involving both the customer and the organization."

"I think I understand. Improvement can happen because the customer pointed out that something could be better or the organizational VP pointed out that profits were dipping, or improvement can happen because a team member finds a new way of working that reduces development time, thereby giving the customer faster results while increasing profits for the organization."

"Exactly. We have two dimensions through which improvement progresses. The organization-customer dimension and the team-responding team-proactive dimensions."

Arjuna was impressed with the figure that Krishna drew on the wall board. He had managed to capture the concept of Continuous Improvement really well.

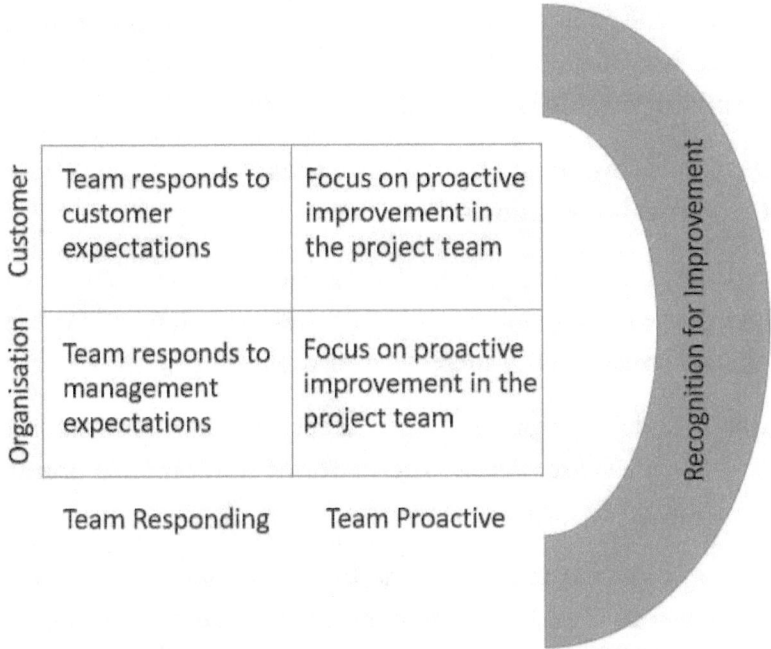

Krishna said, "To get the two main components of this vital sign, we can slice the above figure vertically or horizontally."

Arjuna said, "Let us slice it horizontally for our purpose and get two components."

"Okay. They would then be: Continuous Improvement – Customer Perspective and Continuous Improvement – Internal Organization Perspective."

Continuous Improvement | 219

"Right. We now have two components of this vital sign."

Krishna said, "The manifestations of these two components would be identical, albeit looked at from two different perspectives."

He continued, "First of all, both the customer and management should perceive that the project team has a focus on proactive improvement. Do they come up with improvement ideas of their own, and do they implement them successfully? Do team members actively participate in the generation of new ideas that could improve the solution and productivity and profitability? Are there processes for seeking and formalizing improvement ideas within the team?"

"Okay this is one of the manifestations, I suppose? One on the proactive vertical dimension?"

"Right. The second one is regarding the response of the team. How well does the team respond to customer and management expectations? Does this response quality increase over the life of the project?"

Arjuna said, "I suppose there needs to be a process to assess improvement ideas for value to the customer and organization in terms of better solution or costs vs benefits."

Krishna said, "Correct. And one key thing here to note is that the team, the customer and management need to be continuously on the look-out to identify and adopt new technologies and approaches for improved solutions."

He continued, "Also, improvements are planned and agreed with the customer or management as the case may be. And then the customer or management is involved in identifying expected outcomes and prioritizing Continuous Improvement opportunities."

Krishna said, "Then, there needs to be a way to formally understand that the customer or management is satisfied with the outcomes arising from the execution of improvement plans."

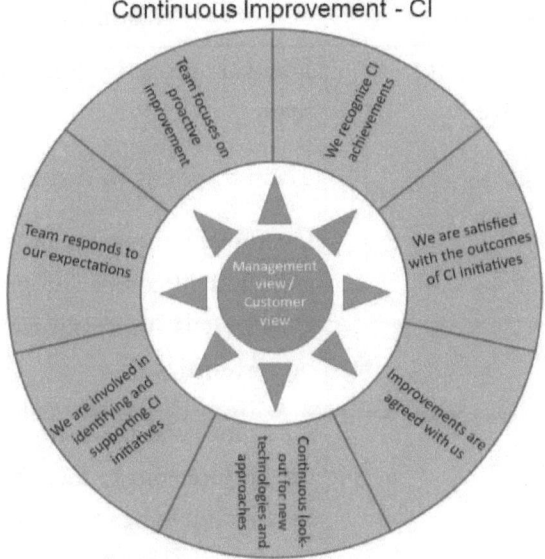

Krishna continued, "One key thing to remember is that the improvement ideas are implemented like formal projects with defined goals and success criteria, and once implemented their benefits are tracked."

"Okay. Have we got all the manifestations of the two components?"

"One additional thing. There must be recognition of the efforts at Continuous Improvement. Both the customer and management must evolve processes to recognize this formally. Otherwise the enthusiasm for Continuous Improvement may be lost."

He said, "Arjuna, can you summarize what we discussed?"

"Okay. Here it is."

Components	Manifestations
Continuous Improvement – customer perspective	Focus on proactive improvement in the team
	Team responds to customer expectations
	Customer is involved in identifying expected outcomes and prioritizing Continuous Improvement opportunities
	Customer and the team are continuously on the look-out to identify and adopt new technologies and approaches for an improved solution
	Improvements are planned and agreed with the customer
	Customer is satisfied with the outcomes arising from the execution of improvement plans
	Customer recognition of Continuous Improvement
Continuous Improvement – internal organization perspective	Focus on proactive improvement in the team
	Team responds to management expectations
	Management is involved in identifying expected outcomes and prioritizing Continuous Improvement opportunities

Components	Manifestations
	Management and the team are continuously on the look-out to identify and adopt new technologies and approaches for an improved solution
	Improvements are planned and agreed with the management
	Management is satisfied with the outcomes arising from the execution of improvement plans
	Management provides recognition for Continuous Improvement

Chapter 8
Programs

Arjuna was feeling thrilled. He had detailed all the six vital signs of projects. He now could forecast the outcomes of all the projects within his program whenever he chose to do so. Also, if his customer at any time wanted to know how the projects were progressing, this framework could be applied.

His elation showed when he next went to meet Krishna. Krishna was meditating in his office when Arjuna walked in. His meditation disturbed, Krishna opened his eyes and looked at Arjuna.

He said, "You seem to be in a great mood today."

"I am. I have finished detailing out all the vital signs of a project."

Krishna smiled. He said, "Well, you are young. Yes, you may have detailed out all the vital signs of projects. You can now assess the health of the projects within your program."

"But?"

"But, what about your program itself? How will you know if the overall program is healthy? The customer finally will judge the entire program, not individual projects. How will Yudhishthira assess the health of your program?"

Arjuna's face fell. "Oh, my God! I had not thought about this at all."

"Don't feel depressed. It's okay. Not many people can think about the situation they are in from within."

Arjuna asked, "What should I do?"

Krishna asked, "Arjuna, tell me. You have led programs before. What is the difference between a project and a program?"

Arjuna said, "I have only led smaller programs before. But, what I know is that a program is a collection of projects working toward a common goal."

"Is that all? What did you do as a program manager?"

Arjuna thought, "For one, I coordinated the work of the different projects under the program."

"Okay, what else?"

"I ensured that the interfaces between the projects are articulated, designed and implemented properly."

"Good. And?"

"I ensured that the products developed by the projects presented a common front and interface to the outside world."

"But that is only if the program is delivering a single integrated product. It needn't be so. The program could be delivering a suite of products. Why was the program called a 'program' and not a large project?"

"I think it is because the program did not end with the delivery of the product. It was ongoing."

"Good. But, why was it ongoing?"

Arjuna thought, "I think it was because the organization's strategy required certain outcomes, and the product developed by my program had to support realizing these outcomes."

"Exactly. You have got it perfect. A program is aligned to an organizational strategic objective, unlike a project which delivers logical parts of what is required to meet the objective."

Arjuna said, "Now that you say it, it makes sense."

Krishna said, "Yes. In fact, Yudhishthira told me that you had the makings of a great program manager. You only had to learn the terms!"

Krishna asked, "What else did you observe about the program? How was your interaction with the customer?"

"We had to prove to the customer that the product delivered was helping the customer realize the advantages due to the strategic objective."

"Wonderful. You mean you had to manage the benefits delivered by the program?"

"Right. Benefits and RoI management was the key thing."

Krishna said, "Let us look at Program Kurukshetra and see what the benefits to be delivered are."

Arjuna said, "Well the benefits are:

1. Reduce illegal entry into the city by 95%
2. Increase by 35% customs duty collection from traders entering the city with goods and leaving with cash
3. Deploy defense shields in under three seconds and ensure people are in bomb shelters in under one hour
4. Launch missiles in pre-emptive strikes against enemy missiles at a far enough distance from the city
5. Protect computers and communication systems from cyber warfare by enemies
6. A centralized command center for monitoring and triggering actions across all systems and interfaces to ensure coordinated high-impact actions in time with zero collateral damage."

Krishna said, "You can see how these benefits are different from project goals which are to deliver required software to specifications. You can also see that benefits can be delivered incrementally and not only as the big bang at the end."

He continued, "For example, you need only Gardabhavyuha for the first and second benefit realization (with interfaces to the customs duty collection at the gates of the city). Project Kurmavyuha (cyber security) is also more or less independent, not too much coupled with other projects, though they are all parts of the integrated program. So, benefits 1, 2 and 5 can be delivered and realized ahead of other benefits."

Arjuna said, excited, "But benefits 3, 4 and 6 are closely related (peril detection, action – proactive and defensive and coordinated response with no collateral damage) and hence the corresponding projects need to come together to deliver."

"Exactly. You catch on fast! So, we have three key program attributes that are different from project attributes. First is strategic alignment, second is benefits management and third is coordination and interfaces management. These are the three key things that set a program apart from a project."

"I get it. I have been doing all this."

"Yes. Exactly. And these three areas will clearly result in vital signs of the program."

"Okay."

Krishna continued, "Of course, there are other areas also that matter. For example, stakeholder management."

"But, the program stakeholders will be different from the project stakeholders?"

"Certainly. You are dealing with a higher level of stakeholders. Stakeholders who are looking at delivering and achieving strategic objectives and looking at benefits.

Krishna continued, "In fact, as a program manager you have to think big picture; think customer strategy; think stakeholder benefits; think relationships; and think vision and leadership."

Arjuna asked, "Won't risk management also be one of the areas to look at?"

"Yes. It would. However, you need to clearly distinguish between program and project risks. As program manager you should be concentrating on managing program risks, leaving project risks to the project managers."

Arjuna asked, "And how would you judge whether a risk is a program risk or a project risk?"

Krishna said, "Very simple. Ask yourself these questions: Is the risk affecting RoI or benefits delivery? Is it affecting organizational strategy delivery? Is it a risk based on market/environmental factors? Is it affecting project output integration with system? Is the risk affecting financial performance? If the answer to some of these questions is yes, you are probably dealing with a program risk, and you should be up in arms against it."

"Okay. I now understand. And in a similar fashion, I can manage program change too?"

"Correct."

Krishna continued, "And as the person managing benefits, you should be more aware of the financials of the program than a project manager would the financials of a project."

"Naturally."

Krishna said, "So you see that the areas of risk management, change management, financial management and others are similar to that in project management but qualitatively different."

"Okay."

Krishna continued, "The next area is the actual program life cycle management."

"Oh?"

Krishna said, "Program lifecycle management has to be flexible, adaptable and responsive. It is implementing the areas of strategy alignment, benefits management and the other areas we talked about on an ongoing basis."

Krishna continued, "And these areas also contribute to program management vital signs. So, you can see that the study of vital signs of a program is a fairly large area and needs separate attention."

Arjuna said, "In fact, now when I think back, Yudhishthira's reviews of my program were always based on these areas! He knew what it took to make a program successful."

"Yes. He is a very competent person."

Krishna continued, "Anyway, we can take program management up and look at the vital signs of a program later. I think you should now consolidate your project vital sign assessment techniques. We can think of program management later. For now, we will continue to rely on the experience and expertise of people like Yudhishthira for monitoring health at a program level. Maybe we will get him involved when we get to adding program vital signs to the framework."

"Okay."

Chapter 9

Conclusions

Vital Signs of Agile Projects

Arjuna sought out Krishna and said, "Krishna, one doubt has been nagging me for some time now."

"What is it?"

"Well, we have the vital signs for projects. We also have thought of a vital sign for the program. But, my concern is this. The vital signs we have distilled out are mainly from non-Agile approach-based projects. Will these same vital signs be valid for Agile projects also?"

Krishna said, "Well, the vital signs will be the same. So, will the components. However, the manifestations will be different."

Arjuna said, "Okay, let us take 'Customer Connect' and look at its components for Agile-based projects."

Krishna said, "Hold it, Arjuna. Make sure you understand the framework you have developed so far, validate this and see how useful it is for you. We can work on Agile-based projects after that. We should ensure that when we start work on that we have the learnings from what we have done so far."

"I agree. Let us meet on this after a month."

"Great. We will then work out the vital signs for Agile-based projects…"

Using the Vital Signs for Forecasting Project Outcomes

Arjuna asked, "Krishna, now that we have these vital signs, how will we use them? How do we forecast the outcomes or the project? I want to use the vital sings to ensure that at any stage of a project, there is good confidence of achieving the project outcomes and the project is healthy."

Krishna said, "Okay. Tell me, Arjuna, what is a project?"

"A project really means a set of practices, carried out by a set of stakeholders for the realizing of certain outcomes."

Krishna said, "Perfect! That is exactly what it is. Putting it another way, a project is about achieving a set of outcomes, interacting with stakeholders and growing the solution through a set of practices."

He then asked, "Arjuna, what are the basic outcomes expected from a project?"

Arjuna thought and answered, "Well, a product delivered to the requirements of the customer, on time, with the expected quality and within estimated cost. This is the ideal situation."

Krishna said, "So the basic outcomes are: Scope, Schedule, Quality and Cost. Right?"

"Right."

"So, you want to know how well the project is doing at any stage, with respect to delivering these outcomes."

"Correct."

Krishna asked, "These are normally measured using metrics like variances, productivity, requirements stability, defect density, cost of quality, Say/Do ratio, etc. But I feel that this is not enough."

Arjuna looked confused.

Krishna said, "These metrics will need to be supplemented with qualitative perspectives of the stakeholders of the project."

Arjuna looked even more confused. He said, "What…"

Krishna said, "Relax. I will explain what I am talking about. Let us take as an example the metric Say/Do ratio. This ratio measures what a team says it will deliver in a space of time against what it actually delivers."

Arjuna said, "Yes, I know this metric. It is commonly used in Agile projects."

"Yes. But it can also be used in conventional projects. This metric is very interesting to analyze. Let us say that a team commits to delivering, say, 30 story points in an iteration, but goes on to deliver 40. This project metric will show deep green status indicating a healthy project at first glance, since the team seems to be delivering beyond commitments."

"What is the problem then?"

"Let us look at a few possible perspectives on this:

Customer: These guys are good. They are delivering well over their commitments

OR

While that is good, maybe these guys keep under-committing just so that they can project their project status as green on a sustained basis.

Delivery management: Why are these fellas delivering more than what is committed? May be the team is over-skilled? I should be pulling out some experienced people from the team and replace them with less senior engineers.

Project manager: This is good. I am pushing the team and giving them stretch targets. Customer will be delighted, and I will get a good name with my managers if we continue this way.

Team member: We are working day and night just for the project manager's glory? This project may not carry much weight for my next career move. So, why should I sacrifice my family life and slog it out like this with no end in sight?

See the difference in the perspectives between the different stakeholders? The same green status shown by the metric Say/Do is generating all these reactions. The quantitative metric should, therefore, be viewed jointly with stakeholder perspectives from their respective vantage points."

Krishna continued, "Remember, we had talked about achieving not just the quality of the product alone, but also the quality of the development practices? In this case above, even though we had a green metric, the customer experience may not necessarily be great, management may think they have over-staffed the project, and team members may be losing motivation. So, if the project reviewers went with just the quantitative metrics to assess overall health, they would miss all these leading indicators under the surface that there is a time bomb ticking."

"So, are you saying that we need a formal mechanism to periodically capture these stakeholder perspectives?"

"Exactly."

"What kind of mechanism can we have?"

Krishna said, "We need a mechanism that seeks inputs that connect to the vital signs from the key stakeholders. This is where the underlying vital signs come into force. The perspectives of the stakeholders can, for example, be got through the responses to a set of questions either in a survey or in an interview. These questions are spawned from the vital signs, and each question response will feed into the health status of one or more project outcomes."

He continued, "The health of all the vital signs together will indicate the health of the project as a whole and the forecast of achieving outcomes."

Arjuna asked, "How will we use these vital sign statuses and health of the project?"

Krishna said, "From the details of the current health of the project, forecasts can be made about the outcomes of the project."

"Okay, if the health of the project is bad, the outcomes also can be expected to be unsatisfactory?"

"Exactly, unless the project course is changed. So, these forecasts can serve to help correct a wayward project. What poor health of a vital sign indicates is that the practices underlying that vital sign are unsatisfactory."

"That's true."

"By the way, in addition to the classic four outcomes of Scope, Schedule, Quality and Cost, good practices, indicated by healthy vital signs, will result in the positive realization for three other outcomes."

"What are these?"

Krishna said, "These outcomes relate to the stakeholders we talked about earlier. The three key stakeholders are the investor in the project (who is represented by the delivery management), the recipient or the beneficiary of the project (the customer) and the provider (the project team). These three stakeholders, each, expect an outcome over and above the four outcomes we mentioned above."

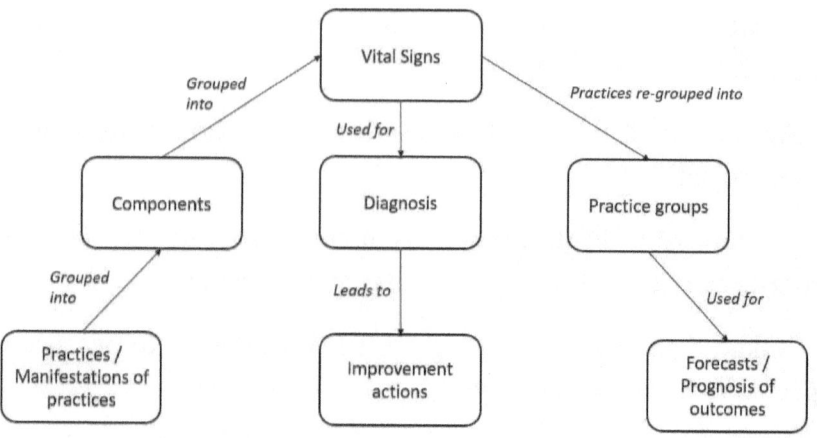

Krishna continued, "These outcomes are: Management Expectations, Customer Experience and Team Satisfaction. The long-term success measurement of a project will depend on these outcomes being satisfactory."

He continued, "Remember, each vital sign value is a result of following a respective set of practices. These practices then contribute to these three outcomes."

"What are these practices?"

Customer Engagement Practices, People Practices, Engineering Practices, Execution Practices, Delivery Organization Practices and Continuous Improvement Practices."

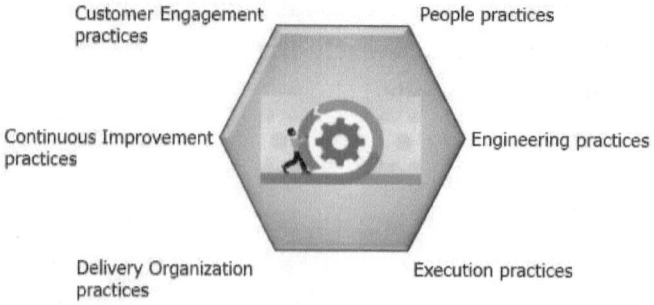

He continued, "The four result outcomes of Scope, Schedule, Quality and Cost are also dependent on these practices. Issues seen in the practices can indicate which stage of the PDCA cycle (Plan, Do, Check/Act) problems exist in. It can also indicate if there are problems with the project environment."

Arjuna asked, "The three stakeholder outcomes and the earlier result outcomes (scope, schedule, quality & cost) are all dependent on the correct implementation of these practices?"

"Exactly."

Arjuna said, "Okay. I get it."

Krishna continued, "So, any forecast that tells you that a project has, for example, issues with the Customer Experience outcome, should tell you also where exactly, in what practice, the problem is: Is it in the customer engagement practices, or is it in people practices, etc. This way, forecasts are made actionable."

Arjuna asked, "So, based on a survey of the key stakeholders of a project, their perspectives can be got, which will then indicate the health of the project with reference to the six vital signs. Based on the current health of the project and the status of the vital signs, forecasts can be made as to the success of the four result outcomes – Scope, Schedule, Quality and Cost – and the three stakeholder outcomes – Customer Experience, Team Satisfaction and Management Expectations."

"Perfect. Remember, to be actionable, the forecasts should indicate the practice where there is an issue. Also, the forecasts should indicate where there is a serious discord in the perspectives between different stakeholders."

"Of course."

Krishna said, "So, a forecast will have a prognosis and a diagnosis of the problems. It will also indicate where the problem is and what the disconnect is, where it exists, between the perspectives of the situation of the different stakeholders."

Krishna continued, "The confidence level of each forecast will depend mainly on how well represented the stakeholders were in the survey. A 360-degree response to the survey – where all the key stakeholders have responded will have the highest confidence level. The confidence level decreases if some of the stakeholders have not given their perspective."

Arjuna said, "Okay. Now I understand how the vital signs can be used."

Krishna said, "Once a project team is furnished with a forecast, they can work on specific practices identified as improvement areas identified in the forecasts, investigate "disconnects" between stakeholder perspectives and devise & implement improvement actions based on the above."

Krishna continued, "Of course, this is one way to implement the process. There could be other equally effective ways."

"They can then wait for a period and do the health analysis again to see how well they are improving."

"This is good. I can use this for my projects. I will develop or look for a tool that implements these concepts."

Chapter 10
Epilogue

Thus, in the space of slightly over three months, Arjuna, with the help of Krishna, was able to put together a comprehensive framework to assess the health of the projects under the Kurukshetra Program and thus forecast their outcomes.

The defense department of Hastinapura had wanted the two competing organizations, the Pandavas and the Kauravas, to demonstrate, during the development process, an ongoing assurance of achieving the desired outcomes at the end of the program. The framework developed by Arjuna was designed to do exactly this.

In addition, the framework facilitated Arjuna to understand the health and status of the projects under his program and take corrective action where needed.

The framework thus served two purposes.

The framework defined the health of a project through the diagnosis of a set of vital signs – a set of high-level indicators of the underlying health of a project. The six vital signs are: Customer Connect, Goal-Focused Team, Engineering Excellence, Execution Excellence, Engaged Management and Continuous Improvement. The health of these vital signs was predicated on a set of manifestations or practices, grouped together as components under each vital sign. Vital signs and components are universal. However, the manifestations may be specific to types of projects – for example: Agile vs non-Agile.

For example, one of the components under the vital sign "Customer Connect" is "Operational Connect with Customer" and the manifestations (or practices) of it are given in the table.

Operational Connect with Customer	Regular communication with the customer exists regarding project status – weekly, monthly, quarterly
	Project-related communication exists between project hierarchy and the customer at multiple levels
	Customer escalations are dealt with swiftly and objectively, and preventive steps are taken to avoid recurrence
	The team is involved in analyzing escalations and implementing preventive actions for the future
	Management support is effective in assisting/supporting project escalations

Let us take one of the manifestations: Customer escalations are dealt with swiftly and objectively, and preventive steps are taken to avoid recurrence.

What the framework asserts is that if this practice (and other practices in the table) is being implemented properly and consistently, there is a very high chance that the Operational Connect with Customer is good at that moment. If, similarly, the practices under the other components of Customer Connect are also being implemented properly, there is a high chance that the vital sign of "Customer Connect" is healthy. If, similarly, the other vital signs are also healthy, it will be possible to make a positive forecast of the outcomes of the project.

The key outcomes about which forecasts can be made based on the vital signs are: Scope, Schedule, Quality and Cost and the stakeholder outcomes of Management Expectations, Customer Experience and Team Satisfaction.

Arjuna realized very early on that metrics-based, quantitative approaches to assessing the impact of the correct implementation of the practices that go toward making vital signs would not give the complete picture. A "green" metric (or a "red" or "amber" one) may throw up different reactions from different stakeholders. Stakeholders will have different perspectives about how well the project is going and if it is going the way that particular stakeholder wants.

Acting on this realization, Arjuna also wisely built a tool that allowed for capturing a 360-degree view of the project based on his selection of stakeholder vantage points as below:

- The recipient of the benefits (The Customer)
- The investor in the project (The Management of the Delivery Organization)
- The providers of the benefits (The Project-In-Charge and the Project Team)

Each stakeholder's perspective is assessed using his response to a survey that seeks inputs about the various manifestations and practices under each vital sign.

The overall result of this 360-degree assessment would give Arjuna a set of leading indicators to what could be going wrong (or right) and where corrective actions need to be taken.

The Kurukshetra Program was making good progress. Teams from the customer would periodically descend on the projects, like wolves on the fold, to check on the status and to get an assurance of successful outcomes.

The experience was very harrowing for Arjuna the first two or three times this happened. Arjuna could present to the customer a set of metrics-based indicators, showing all the colors of the rainbow. The metrics indicated that some projects were not making good progress.

There were also inputs from the customer representatives of the projects that they were not happy with the progress.

The Kauravas, on the other hand, seemed to have a much better time with the wolves. Most of their projects were green, and Shakuni and others were able to convince the customer that they would be able to deliver on all outcomes successfully.

Arjuna and his project managers had to put their teams on overdrive. They had to fix the issues that were thrown up by the customer during their visits. Team morale started dropping slowly. Yudhishthira and others of the management team started wondering whether they would be able to recoup what they had invested in the project. The customer started wondering whether they would have a good experience and a stable product from the Pandavas.

By the third time the customer team came to assess the status, Arjuna was ready. Using his vital signs framework and tool, Arjuna was ready to administer the 360-degree survey. Using this, he could prove that his projects were improving and they were implementing all the right practices to ensure satisfactory outcomes.

It was the Kauravas who were squirming now. Their initial successes seemed like a dream now. Though their metrics were still indicating greens all around, the customers of the different projects were increasingly reporting dissatisfaction. The Kauravas were not able to fathom why. They put pressure on the teams, and many of their team members left, unable to handle the stress. A couple of top managers also resigned.

The customer asked the Kauravas also to implement a framework and tool similar to the one the Pandavas were using.

But, it was too late for them…

At the end of one year, the defense department was convinced that the Kauravas could not deliver. They terminated the contract, and the Kauravas went into a collective blame-game environment.

Sanjaya said, "Sir, we have lost the Kurukshetra battle. The customer has terminated our contract. The Pandavas have won."

Dhrtarashtra asked, "Sanjaya, what went wrong? Why did we reach this situation?"

"Duryodhana depended too much on Shakuni and too heavily on the status reporting and forecasting based only on quantitative information that Shakuni was comfortable with. So, they were not able to sense some of the underlying issues early on."

Sanjaya continued, "The main reason for the Pandavas' success was that Arjuna had implemented a framework, based on which he was able to assess the underlying health of his projects from different vantage points. In fact, he got a 360-degree view of his projects. This gave him leading indications as to what is likely to go wrong and which practice was in need of repair to correct the trend. The vital signs framework and the tool that implemented it was one of the key reasons for the success of the Pandavas."

"What are Duryodhana and others going to do now?"

Sanjaya said, "Well, some of these top managers will need to leave. We will try to salvage our engineering teams for other projects."

Dhrtarashtra said, "Poor Duryodhana. I thought that he had it in him to see this program through."

"He is, no doubt, good. But, unless you follow the right path, success will elude you."

Dhrtarashtra said, "Did you know that our chairman, Bhishma, is in hospital? The poor man could not take this news. He seems to have had a heart attack."

"Really?"

"You know that Bhishma was once Yudhishthira's manager? And Arjuna was a trainee in Bhishma's team many years ago?"

"I did not know that."

That evening saw Yudhishthira and Arjuna visiting Bhishma in hospital.

Yudhishthira asked, "Sir, how are you feeling?"

"Not too good. I don't think I will survive this. It is only a matter of days, if not hours."

Yudhishthira and Arjuna felt uncomfortable. They uttered some sympathetic noises and tried to cheer Bhishma on.

Bhishma turned to Yudhishthira. "You have a good man in Arjuna here. Make sure you employ him well. He is ready for bigger responsibilities."

Arjuna felt embarrassed. He asked Bhishma, "Sir, do you have any advice for me?"

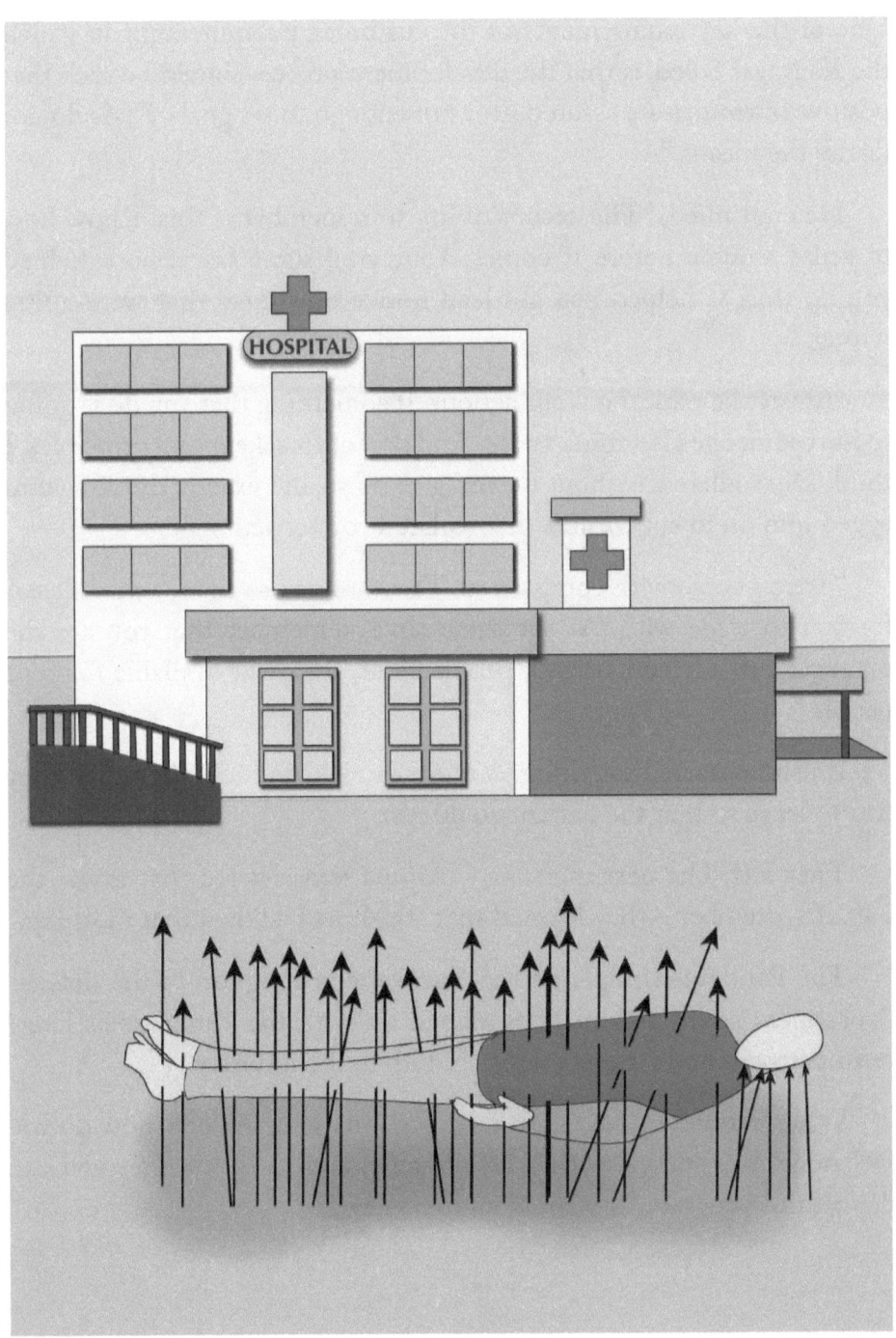

"Well, Arjuna, you have learned a lot in this program, Kurukshetra. One of the key requirements of the customer, a requirement in which the Kauravas failed, is that the development process should be such that positive outcomes are assured. It is not enough to set goals. Ends do not justify the means."

He continued, "The second thing to remember is this. Know how to sense trouble before it comes. Your vital signs framework helped you do this. It helped you get lead notice on things that were going wrong."

"Always be ethical in your actions. If something that you do is going to hurt someone else, think twice. And do not forsake moral principles. I think Duryodhana, without meaning to do so, did exactly this. Shakuni egged him on to cut corners that violated correct action."

"Treat people with compassion. They are not 'so many tons of steel' for you to trade with. At the same time, remember that you are the manager, not a friend, of your people. And, always be available for your people."

Bhishma started coughing. A nurse came in and told them that they had to leave so that the patient could rest.

They left. The next morning – Arjuna remembered that it was the 23rd of December – they learned that Bhishma had died that morning.

The Pandavas completed the Kurukshetra Program to the defense department's satisfaction. They signed on with the Pandavas as long-term partners, and Arjuna's fame shot up in the industry.

When Arjuna met Krishna next, Krishna said, "Arjuna, how do you feel now? You started with a lot of self-doubt as to whether you can deliver this program. You could and you have."

Arjuna said, "Krishna, I could not have done it without you. The concept of the framework of vital signs, which you helped me put together, was the key differentiator between us and the Kauravas."

Krishna said, "I am happy to have helped. I feel it is my duty to help whenever the high standards of program and project management are diluted. I will be available to coach you whenever you need me."

"Thank you, Krishna."

Sanjaya said, "Well, Bhishma has passed away. You may get to become the chairman of the Kauravas."

Dhrtarashtra asked, "Can we become like the Pandavas?"

"You will have to strive hard. Remember, the Pandavas had Arjuna, and Krishna to coach him."

"Of course."

Sanjaya said, "It is my firm belief that wherever there is the coach Krishna and the supreme manager Arjuna, there will always be win-win for all stakeholders, positive outcomes and benefits, RoI and correct action."

||wherever there is the coach krishna and the supreme manager arjuna, there will always be win-win for all stakeholders, positive outcomes and benefits, roi and correct action||

Are You Ready to Implement the Framework?

Well, here we are in the real world beyond the end of the epic...

We hope you enjoyed reading the book and virtually participating in the discovery of the framework by Arjuna aided by Krishna.

If you recall, in Chapter 9, "Conclusions," Arjuna was starting to look for a tool that implemented the project health framework. We have just such a tool for you to explore called proFes360™. proFes360™ is an on-line project health assessment tool available for free on our website: pm-powerconsulting.com.

Here is a brief introduction to proFes360™ and what it can do for you:

proFes360™ seeks to capture 360-degree project stakeholder perspectives through a questionnaire, based on which it automatically draws inferences and forecasts with an associated degree of confidence. proFes360™ also identifies potential areas to improve any disconnects between the perspectives of various stakeholders. An example of a disconnect is that the project team may think that since they are working very hard to meet every requirement, customer experience should, by default, be great. The customer may think otherwise – that the team, in her view, is not flexible enough to meet her intent but focusing only on the explicitly-stated requirements.

The assessment of perspectives from different stakeholders' vantage points provides a valuable qualitative insight and can be used in conjunction with other quantitative metrics and forecasts. proFes360™ is an early warning system for potential RED flags enabling more effective remedial actions earlier on.

proFes360™'s design and inference engine are based on the essence of years of PM Power experience in guiding projects and delivery organizations. The proFes360™ approach and the tool itself have been validated in a number of projects and teams. proFes360™ continues to "learn" and improve as its usage spreads – so, while you get valuable insights to your project health, proFes360™ also learns from your project. Your project data is fully secure, protected by a Non-Disclosure Agreement agreed upfront between you and PM Power. Please go ahead and avail the benefits of using proFes360™ – it is simple, light-weight and can be completed in as little as fifteen minutes per stakeholder. And it works for Agile as well as non-Agile projects.

Here is a special offer for you as the buyer of our book: Visit pm-powerconsulting.com and sign-up for using proFes360™ for one or more of your projects – for free. You also stand a chance of winning a 1-hour consultation at no charge with the author of this book to better understand proFes360™ forecasts for one of your projects and the actions that you need to take for successful project outcomes.

So, what are you waiting for?

Appendix A
Making of the Book and the Tool

How the Book was written and the Tool developed is a story in itself. We cannot tell it all here but here are some snippets. Many PM Powerians contributed significantly to both and they made the journey all the more fun and memorable...

Ananth with his wealth of experience as the original creator of the project health framework and the driving force behind its continuous improvement and application in customer engagements; he played the consultant and reviewer roles to perfection.

Gayatri with her boundless enthusiasm and energy brought in loads of project data of various kinds to test the tool – a significant help with validating the Tool approach and its tuning; she is always our cheerleader in everything new that we attempt – when in self-doubt, we go to her to consult and come away re-charged!

Sivaguru, the go-to man for ideas who always prodded us to think beyond what we thought was possible; supported us significantly in enhancing the Tool and its positioning; he patiently tested the initial wobbly versions of the Tool and gave us solid suggestions to improve; he reached out to prospects and customers for Tool trials and validation.

Srinivasan, the only person who can think faster than Excel! Reviewer par excellence – we owe him a great deal for his multiple, fine toothcomb reviews of the Book; he pointed out the sensitivities, nuances and the due diligence required while writing a business novel; his immense experience and insights into the dynamics of project leadership and managing delivery were key in getting the  Tool take off from concept to reality in double quick time.

Vasudev, referred by us as the Eagle Eye as nothing escapes his critical review, not only at the content level but language, font and presentation levels; upon seeing Vasu approach a review, words panic and self-organize to dot their "i's" and cross their "t's" – all by themselves; Vasu provided many useful inputs for the Tool and helped enhance our pitch presentations as well.

Veeraraaghavan (JV), our font of knowledge on the epic; he indulged us in our sometimes, cavalier treatment of the Mahabharata characters; JV conducted some intense critical reviews of both the framework and the complete Book; stirred us up from smugness and made us humble again with the revelation of some glaring lacunae.

Vishu Hegde, whose sheer presence is energizing; he brought in a very different perspective in his in-depth reviews of the Book; uncovered issues we would have never caught and suggested improvements which we would have never thought of; we are also ever grateful to him for getting timely inputs for the Book from industry leaders.

Last, though not the least in importance, Sivakumar (ShivK), the "product owner" of the book and the author's mentor. He took over the ownership of the book at a critical stage and made sure that it reflected the project health framework truly. When the author was stuck or "blocked" at some point, he was always there to provide the sentence or paragraph to "unblock" him. It was he who engaged the publisher and the artist for illustrations and brought it all together.

Appendix B
The Project Health Framework

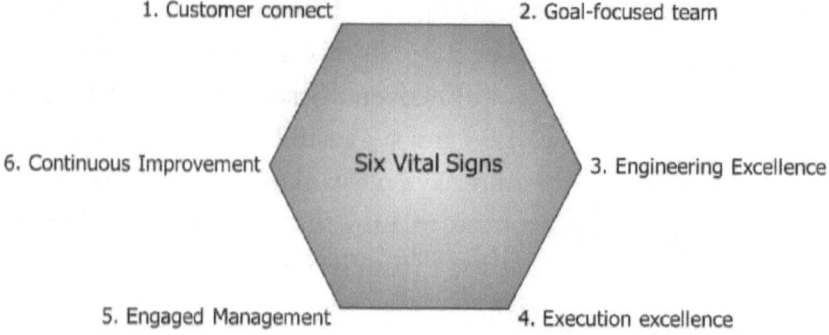

Vital Sign → Components → Manifestations

Vital Sign: Customer Connect

Components	Manifestations
Contractual Commitment Management	The team clearly understands contractual commitments made to the end customer and the consequences of not meeting them
	The team understands contractual commitments made by their organization to its customer
	Project plan is reviewed for meeting contractual commitments

Components	Manifestations
Rigor in Change Management	Changes to customer requirements are captured formally in a comprehensive manner
	Impact of changes is analyzed by the team and possible scenarios for accommodating the changes are discussed with the customer to reach a common understanding and decisions
	Changes in commitments and objectives and the resource requirements are discussed with all stakeholders to arrive at a consensus
	Changes in requirements are factored into the solution design and implemented effectively to meet the revised commitments and objectives
Operational Connect with Customer	Regular communication with the customer exists regarding project status – weekly, monthly, quarterly
	Project-related communication exists between project hierarchy and the customer at multiple levels
	Customer escalations are dealt with swiftly and objectively, and preventive steps are taken to avoid recurrence
	The team is involved in analyzing escalations and implementing preventive actions for the future
	Management support is effective in assisting/supporting project escalations

Components	Manifestations
Actionable Customer Satisfaction Measurement	Customer satisfaction is measured to gain insight to customer perception of performance at appropriate intervals and checkpoints
	Multiple dimensions of customer and user satisfaction are measured: e.g., efficacy of deliverables, project performance, relationship strength, team capability, transactional effectiveness
	Customer satisfaction data is analyzed to identify improvement actions that have measurable impact on project performance
	The team seeks customer feedback on an ongoing basis during the project
	Customer satisfaction is also sensed through inter-personal interactions between the customer and the team
Product and Business Domain Insight	Team has the required opportunities to develop their product and business domain knowledge
	Team has acquired the required level of product and business domain knowledge
	Team demonstrates product and domain knowledge through timely identification of unstated needs
	Customer recognizes our team's ability to provide product & business domain insights

Components	Manifestations
Partnership with Customer	Common engagement vision exists as the foundation for partnership
	Agreed strategies are in place to realize the engagement vision
	The team possesses the ability to realize the engagement vision over time
	Engagement with the customer exists at multiple levels of hierarchy to enable partnership
	Visible progress is made in the project to realize vision/promote partnership
	Partnership benefits are realized and acknowledged publicly

Vital Sign: Goal focused team

Component	Manifestations
Clarity and alignment of individual goals	Relationship between project goals and individual performance goals is discussed and agreed up front
	Relationship between work targets and project goals is well-understood
	Individual project performance has a significant bearing on overall performance

Component	Manifestations
Well-equipped team	Provision of project-specific training, mentoring and multi-skilling of team members including the Project Manager and Leads
	Team-building activities in the project
	Coaching the team to achieve project goals
	Team responds well to a coaching style of management
Team work	Project environment fosters open disagreement
	Conflicts are resolved effectively
	Mutual encouragement within team
	Proactive assistance within team
	Information sharing in the project
	Ownership and a sense of urgency
Learning team	Project experiences are captured and analyzed to identify lessons learned
	Project learns from other projects and shares learning with other projects
	Project exploits re-use
	Project learns from sources external to the organization
	Scope for experimentation

Component	Manifestations
	Application of learning for improved performance (efficiency & effectiveness in achieving project goals)
	Organization fosters a learning culture
Motivated self	Understanding of individual differences in motivation
	Actions are taken to address factors for individual motivation
	Clarity of career path and ownership by individual
	Facilitation of project manager for individual career progression
	The desire to overcome hurdles and obstacles to be successful
	Effective organizational enablers exist for individual career progression
Motivation in the project context	Team involvement in solution development and validation
	Team participation in project decision making
	Learning opportunity in the project for individuals
	Celebrating even small successes.
	Individuals multi-skill effectively to meet commitments
	The team goes the extra mile to meet commitments

Vital Sign: Engineering Excellence

Component	Manifestations
Understanding requirements	Adequate domain expertise exists in the team to understand the intended product requirements
	Adequate domain expertise exists in the team to understand non-functional requirements and elicit requirements that may be implicit
	Visibility of requirement analysis & clarifications to stakeholders
	Healthy dialogue is established with the customer/product owner for timely clarification of requirements
	List of requirements and their inter-relationships are documented and agreed upon
	Requirement priorities are clearly established and understood
	Requirements are met in working software frequently to validate the team's understanding and unearthing unstated needs
Sound design, development & testing capability	Adequate technical expertise exists in the project development / test environment to meet project goals
	Team follows established standards and practices in design, development and testing
	Adequate technical expertise exists in design, development and testing tools & techniques employed in the project

Component	Manifestations
	Adequate technical expertise exists in supporting tools (configuration management, source control, test management etc.)
	Technical environment for development / testing / validation is stable and well-supported
	Project judiciously adopts new technologies to improve capability to deliver
Robust verification and validation	Review of engineering documentation and code are carried out in spirit by the right people
	Interim outputs of deliverables are created and verified internally prior to seeking customer feedback
	Product components from external sources are validated and accepted
	Test strategy adequately addresses the functional requirements
	Test strategy adequately addresses technical / non-functional requirements
	Prototypes are created to validate requirements and the soundness of the architecture
	Development and test environments are adequate to support the verification and validation activities effectively
	Customer's criteria and process for verifying and validating the deliverables is understood

Component	Manifestations
Architecture aspects addressed effectively	Architecture related expertise is adequate in the project
	Chosen architecture meets the requirements in an optimal way and is validated early in the lifecycle
	Architecture enables re-use
	Architecture is reviewed by a panel of experts and architectural risks identified
Achieving Technical Quality Requirements	Architecture and design address product technical quality requirements
	Skills and infrastructure (tools, processes and techniques) are adequate to measure product technical quality.
	Technical quality baselines are created for existing code prior to enhancements and the extent of improving existing code is determined
	Benchmark technical quality requirements for the critical components are established.
	Critical components of the product/solution are built to meet the technical quality requirements.
	Overall product's / solution's technical quality is measured as early as possible to enable meeting the technical quality requirements.
Engineering Practices – Re-use, Tools & Automation	Re-using from other projects
	Contributing to re-use

Component	Manifestations
	Code quality verification is achieved by fully exploiting tools
	Unit testing effectiveness & coverage are achieved through use of tools
	Smoke test scenarios are scripted for automation and are executed when required
	Regression test scenarios are scripted for automation and are executed when required
	Build management practices and tooling are effective in supporting integrity of components and agility requirements of releases
	Configuration management practices and tooling are effective in supporting integrity of the components and enabling effective build management
	Test environment set-up is automated
	Test data population is automated

Vital Sign: Execution Excellence

Component	Manifestations
Clarity of project goals and success criteria – short-term and long-term	Project's purpose and Business Case are well documented and available for the team
	Customer milestones (short term and long term) are well-understood

Component	Manifestations
	There is common understanding between the customer and the team on the definition of deliverables for each milestone
	There is recognition for meeting the goals successfully
	Impact on stakeholders of failure to meet goals is well understood by the team
Estimates reflect capability to deliver	Inputs to estimation include functional & non-functional requirements and it is done by people with the required expertise
	Size is estimated based on the product scope and the nature of work
	Effort, cost and duration are derived from size with appropriate considerations for product attributes, platform attributes, tools used and people capability
	Past data from the project and the organization are used appropriately to derive predictable estimates
	Estimates are realistic
	Estimation assumptions are documented and tracked throughout the project for appropriate actions if they turn out to be false
	Estimates are agreed upon among stakeholders as appropriate and are used to validate ability to deliver on the commitments

Component	Manifestations
Adaptive integrated plans	Plans exist to address requirements and project goals
	Plans have resilience to meet project goals within tolerance levels
	Internal milestones are well-defined and granular to meet short-term customer milestones
	Progressive elaboration of activities is practiced and is accepted by stakeholders
	Project plans identify dependencies (upstream & downstream) and are shared with appropriate stakeholders
	Project plans include review points for progress assessment
	Project plan provides for review of deliverables
	Trigger conditions are identified which require re-planning
	Plans are revised when risks materialize or when unforeseen events occur
	Planning and tracking are well-supported through the right tools
	Plans are independently reviewed initially and when significant changes occur
	Plans are adapted to incorporate new technologies and approaches and the required multi-skilling

Component	Manifestations
Timely resourcing of talent, tools, environment	Pipeline for resource requirements is known adequately in advance
	Resource fulfilment meets project requirements
	Project ownership of staffing and other resources required for the project
	Provisioning for the tools and the operating environment is speedy and well-supported
	Operating environments are stable and well-supported
	Adequate expertise is available in appropriate use of tools
	Resource fulfilment meets project requirements including multi-skilling to enable adoption of new technologies and approaches
Visibility of progress toward goals, understanding of drivers and course correction	Deliverables are reviewed progressively at appropriate periodicity
	Project progress is tracked against the plan with respect to short-term and long-term goals
	External dependencies identified in the plan are monitored on a regular basis

Component	Manifestations
	Resources / baselines from external sources (customer, partner, sub-contractor etc.) are validated before acceptance
	Project re-planning occurs when the trigger conditions are met
	Project progress and reviews are transparent and involve key team members
	Progress review and course correction activities happen at multiple levels in the organization
Proactive risk management at different organization levels	Risks are identified with respect to risk sources applicable to the project (such as product requirements, scope, people, resources, assumptions, dependencies etc.)
	Risks are prioritized and appropriate risk responses developed
	Risk responses are acted upon - in project planning and execution
	Risks are identified and managed throughout the lifecycle of the project
Project budget and tracking	Allocated budget and its components for the project are well-understood
	Expenses are tracked against the budget and are within acceptable limits

Vital Sign: Engaged Management

Component	Manifestations
Management takes action to remove impediments and provide resources	Team members are able to escalate issues to management in a timely manner
	Management's internal reviews of the project are effective
	Management adopts a consultative approach in making customer commitments
	Management facilitates provisioning of necessary resources including funds for timely and speedy removal of impediments
	Management removes impediments in systemic manner (as opposed to just addressing it as a transaction)
Management involvement in project and interest in the team.	Management fosters a project environment that balances task orientation and people orientation
	Management takes an active interest in the project and understands the team's challenges
	Management is effective in addressing project issues balancing stakeholder needs and adopts a facilitative approach
	Management participates in team activities as required

Component	Manifestations
Management connects with customer management and brings insight to the team	Management connects formally and informally with the customer management at all levels
	Management effectively represents the organization and project interests in interactions with the customer
Management sets, promotes and supports the team "brand".	Management understands customer expectations and organization's strengths to position the team accordingly with the customer
	Management sponsors the plan to achieve and sustain the team positioning with the customer
	Management is committed to supporting the building and sustenance of the team brand
Management enables the team to perform at a higher level	Management continuously appreciates the team for their performance while pointing to possibilities for higher performance
	Management mentors the team for higher level of performance
	Failure to improve is seen as temporary and leadership encourages the team learn and move forward

Vital Sign: Continuous Improvement

Component	Manifestations
Continuous improvement – customer perspective	Focus on proactive improvement in the team
	Team responds to customer expectations
	Customer is involved in identifying expected outcomes and prioritizing continuous improvement opportunities.
	Customer and the team are continuously on the look-out to identify and adopt new technologies and approaches for an improved solution
	Improvements are planned and agreed with the customer
	Customer is satisfied with the outcomes arising from the execution of improvement plans
	Customer recognition of continuous improvement
Continuous improvement – internal organization perspective	Focus on proactive improvement in the team
	Team responds to management expectations
	Management is involved in identifying expected outcomes and prioritizing continuous improvement opportunities

Component	Manifestations
	Management and the team are continuously on the look-out to identify and adopt new technologies and approaches for an improved solution
	Improvements are planned and agreed with the management
	Management is satisfied with the outcomes arising from the execution of improvement plans
	Management provides recognition for continuous improvement

Appendix C
About PM Power Consulting

PM Power Consulting helps organizations achieve agility in design and delivery of software and services. Founded in 2006, PM Power Consulting is the leader in transformational consulting and coaching, delivered by expert practitioners with decades of experience in building and leading high-performance organizations.

Designed to help organizations win in this era of hyper-competition and digital disruption, PM Power Consulting offers leadership workshops, consulting and coaching in the areas of Agile Transformation, DevOps Consulting, Program & Project Management*, Delivery Excellence, Mindful Leadership, Design Thinking and Technology Adoption.

PM Power Consulting has successfully delivered hundreds of programs to a wide range of organizations including large MNCs, Indian enterprises, global in-house centers (MNC captives), software development companies, innovative start-ups as well as non-profit organizations.

Please visit: www.pm-powerconsulting.com

(*): Includes project health assessments using the framework covered in this book in detail and the online health assessment tool.

About the Author

Paramu Kurumathur (Paramu) is an avid reader of business and technical books. He has been exposed to various project and program management approaches and different technologies over decades. He has been working in the international software services industry and global IT management since 1980.

He is a keen traveler and has visited and stayed in around 40 countries.

His debut novel, *The First Aryan,* is in the process of being published by Penguin Random House.

Paramu is an alumnus of IIT, Madras. [B. Tech. (Aero. Engg.); M. Tech. (Comp. Sc.)]

His interests include project and program management, writing business books and novels, writing limericks and promoting humor as a way of life.

www.ingramcontent.com/pod-product-compliance
Lightning Source LLC
Chambersburg PA
CBHW020730180526
45163CB00001B/184